Lakeland
Dalesfolk

Lakeland Dalesfolk

by W. R. Mitchell

Dalesman Books
1983

Dalesman Publishing Company Ltd
Clapham, via Lancaster.

First published 1983
© W. R. Mitchell, 1983

ISBN: 0 85206 723 2

Phototypeset, printed and bound by Galava Printing Co. Ltd., Nelson, Lancashire

Contents

Illustrations

Drawings by E. Jeffrey. Photographs—J. Hardman (Three Herdwick Men, Blea Tarn Farm); Tom Parker (Hill Top Farm, Stonethwaite Farm); H.L. Bradley (Dunney Beck Farm); collection of Mrs Mary Birkett (John Richardson, farmer sheep-clipping, the Herdwick Men, Seathwaite, Skiddaw House gathering); collection of Mrs F. Birkett (Langdale kitchen, "Boon" clipping in Great Langdale). Cover picture by Molly Partington.

An Introduction

DALESFOLK were always a race apart, with their own quaint ways which could be amusing to strangers, as evidenced by the droll antics of Will Ritson of Wasdale Head and the effect of these on Victorian visitors. "Every parish had a different way of it own," said a dalesman, when I invited him to recall his young days. He had been bemused by recent changes, and observed: "Now it's all of a splutter."

I had been touring the Lakeland Dales with a tape-recorder, urging the veterans among us to tell me fine details of the old way of life before these were forgotten. "What do you remember?" I asked a retired farmer, and he replied: "Hard work, and not so much for it!" He pondered, then remarked: "There's a lot less work done today—and all this tackle to do it wi'!" (In many interviews, scarcely any Cumbrian dialect was used).

I selected the period 1900 to 1935 for special scrutiny. At the dawn of the century, people lived and worked pretty much as their ancestors had done down the long years, and by the mid-1930s social life was changing rapidly as communications with the outside world improved and machinery was available to perform many of the farming tasks which hitherto had depended on the muscles of man and horse. The 1914-18 war had a profound effect on Lakeland life by destroying a host of young men and unsettling those who survived. Within a few years, there was an awesome slump. Yet "when I was young, the world was a heck of sight more content than it is today."

Hard work was taken for granted. In Great Langdale, at a time when a farm man earned about £1 a week, one of the fraternity asked his employer if he could have a day off. "Aye," was the reply, "... but be back for milking toneet." Also in Langdale: "We had to work for anything we got. In summer-time, our shoes were never cold." When visiting the upper valley of the Lune, a now prosperous farmer told me with pride: "I started wi' nowt, an' no-one ever left me owt!"

The working round was ceaselessly demanding, but "everything was done voluntarily in those days." There were the famous "boon days", such as when sheep were to be clipped through communal effort. In the Lyth Valley: "When anyone took over a new farm, the friends and neighbours had a 'boon day' and went along to help. They might plough up the land. Aye—there was one day when I saw 10 pairs of horses yoked up." Those were the days of large families, with plenty of labour available at home. "We shifted from t'shore up into t'hills. It was a biggish farm, wi' a lot o'sheep to it. It was a hard-work spot—up hill, down dale. When we carted muck we had to have two horses in one cart. I remember when we first moved in. One o' t'locals said: 'Well, they wean't need mich help. There's no family fitter—three gurt lads, big as house-ends and strong as waggin'-hosses.'" Before the machines arrived, a Lunesdale farmer had "nobbut a horse and a cart and a sledge and a muck-fork."

The dalesfolk perpetuated an ancient round of activity against a backdrop provided by some of the finest mountains in Britain. It was a farmer at Hartsop who observed: "There's gey little bottom-land i' this part o' t'Lake District. That's t'trouble. Valleys are too narrow, and there's not mich flat in t'bottom. Flattest bit is covered by lake!"

The farmers drew a living mainly from their flocks of stocky Herdwicks. In Langdale: "There's just one thing more beautiful than a nice Herdwick sheep ... and that's a lady, nicely dressed!" Herdwick Billy (William Wilson) called his home near Bassen-thwaite Lake "Herdwick View", and he arranged for pictures of Lakeland's own breed of sheep to be copied on glass and inserted, colourfully, in some of the windows. He once told me: "T'auld fellows were as near self-supporting as possible."

Farmers were characterful to a man. "They were hard nuts to crack, were farmers, and some of them still are!" Slip-shod ways upset them. "They were particular in those days." Wherever possible, they diversified their farming. Near Coniston: "When we came here, everyone had a bit o' corn and a bit o' green crop. Now nobody has nowt. Hardly anybody keeps hens." In this district, a man might work at the quarry and let his wife take care of the small farm, having a "holiday" at haytime. There were "mixed marriages". In Langdale: "Father was a quarryman. Mother was off farming stock."

Dalesfolk did have the capacity to enjoy themselves—when the daily work was done. In Langdale: "We did have some good fun, didn't we? Good clean fun—no badness." Elsewhere in that dale: "We were satisfied with a little. They talk about strong drink; we'd no money to get any drink with, when we were lads. If you got till a dance, you were satisfied."

This book is an unpretentious account of ordinary life as it used to be, as told by the dalesfolk themselves. A host of people have assisted me to recreate incidents from a period which is historically recent, but which now charms us by its quaintness. I thank in

8

particular: Mrs Lucy Bell, Mr and Mrs F. Birkett, Mrs M. Birkett, Rowley Braithwaite, Robert Brownrigg, Mrs Brunskill, Mr and Mrs Stanley Edmondson, Mrs Greenup, Joseph Hayton, John Hind, Mr and Mrs J. Hodgson, Ernest Middleton, Tom Storey, Arthur Wilson, Jonty Wilson, W. Wilson.

Life at Home

A DALEHEAD FARM might be huge, with over 1,000 sheep. "They were mainly little farms in these dales—50 to 60 acres of 'inland' with rights on the fell." The farmer ran a stock of Herdwick sheep; he milked a few Shorthorn cows, rearing calves as replacements. "If they kept horses, they had fewer cattle. You needed a fair amount of grass to keep a horse." At Coniston, "we grew turnips, cabbages, cauliflowers, Brussels sprouts, carrots and beetroots. If we had any oats, we took 'em to t'mill for grinding." Today there are hardly any farms round Coniston. "They've been sold off i' bits."

A farmhouse could be a crowded place, for big families were the rule. "When I was at a farm in Kentmere, there were four sons and two daughters—and they were all at home. It were t'same at another farm in t'valley. Farmer couldn't pay 'em, could he? They only got their clothes an' keep." In Langdale, "I worked at home till I was 33, and I had nowt much in t'bank in them days. A few pounds. But I did manage to take farm over when fadder give ower. He left us a lot of sheep and cattle. I didn't take much hurt in that respect." Also in Langdale: "I used to git a bit o' pocket money, that's all. Eighteen years work—for next to nothing! That's why I left home. As a rule, when one of farmer's family git married, he gave 'em £5 as a wedding present, and that was it!"

A farmer wishing to employ labour went to one of the hiring fairs, held at Whitsuntide and Martinmas. At Ulverston, "lads just stood around on t'side o' t'street. If a farmer thought someone looked like a big lump o' cheap labour, he'd go and see if he could hire him—for as little as he could." At Kendal hirings, "there were scores and scores o' men. They were all standin' round, and farmer would go amang 'em and ax 'em." Some farm men at Kendal attached match stalks or pieces of straw to their caps; "then t'farmers knew where they were to hire, and approached 'em." A good man could afford to be discriminating. "He chose the farmer; it was not just a matter of the farmer choosin' him!"

At Keswick, "we used to hang about in the *Packhorse* yard, or around that spot, where at one time they used to sell milk and

10

butter and eggs on a Saturday. Farm hands from Threlkeld, Borrowdale and Bassenthwaite usually congregated in that area.... They used to barter away at one another, and probably some of 'em weren't taken on just at that time. They stuck out a bit longer. Eventually they accepted—or found another chap. If they were going to be out of a job, they had to take it. 'Oh, it'll do for six months,' a farm man would say. If they didn't get hired, they went on to Cockermouth."

The farm man looked out for a farmer who might provide a good home, with substantial food. "I felt sorry for a lot o' men; they had some blooming bad homes. Some weren't allowed to have their meals wi' t'family. ..I always said it wanted altering. It was slavery, that's what it was. You had to be blooming strong to stick it."

A farm man was employed for a six months' term at an arranged figure, which was paid at the end of the term. The farmer handed his selected man a shilling. "You were fast then, legally fast, same as in t'Army." A young lad from Longsleddale who hired at Kendal was paid £3 for his labours from the end of July until Martinmas. "The highest wage I ever had was £50 for the half year." A Borrowdale lad's first wage, at the age of 13, was £4.10s for six months, and the largest sum he was paid before joining the Forces for the 1914-18 was was £28, by which time "I could do practically anything on a farm."

In Borrowdale, "my father was a farm man at the beginning; and he finished up at the quarry." A lad from Little Langdale who received £8 for the first six months of his working life, and was handed a shilling—"to fasten me"—found he was lucky. "I had three or four good spots. At some farms, men didn't get enough to eat. My brother used to go for the winter months, and I went for the summer months."

Farmers who needed labour often preferred to employ a local lad, from a family they knew well, and ignore the hirings. A Kentmere lad who began work at 13 received £2, "and my keep", for a six months' term. He was employed by his uncle. His pay rose by 10s each half year, and "I finished up at that farm with £6." As uncle had not intended to give him much more, "I told him I was gang to have a change. I knew I could get more at another spot. Old Jack Gilpin, of High Fold, saw me at t'Saturday night. I'd been down in t'village. He said: 'I hear your leaving.' I said: 'Yes.' He said: 'How mich do you want for t'half year?' I said: 'I want £11.' 'Right, I'll give you it. You can start for me when you've had your holidays.' I was 12 month wi' Jack. I got another ten bob off him for second half year."

Another change was considered. "I was ploughing one Saturday morning. The old farmers used to yoke up of a Saturday morning to go to Kendal for their week's proven'. I was ploughing down bi'

11

t'roadside, an' Nathan Gregg and his two sisters came by in t'horse and trap. They stopped. Nathan said: 'I hear thou's leaving.' I said: 'Yes.' He said: 'Will you come to Kentmere Hall and work for us?' I said: 'Aye—I don't mind, if money's reet.' He said: 'I'll gie thee £16 for half year.' I said: 'Reet—I'll be there.' An' that was that!''

Hiring days continued to be held until fairly recent times. At Bampton, "my husband was a farm worker, and in 1922 he earned £1 a week. We married on that. They took ninepence off him for insurance, so I had to go out and work as well." A farmer who visited Ulverston Hirings in 1930 secured the services of a lad for farm work. It was a depressing experience. "The streets were thick with out-of-work men, many of whom had pinched faces. I found a man who said he would work for nothing rather than miss a place where he could have regular food and be able to keep warm; he had almost starved to death in the previous winter.

"He agreed to come for 50 bob, though I raised his wage a lot later. I gave him a bob to fix the bargain. He never went out at nights, unless it was to a local dance, which cost him only a shilling. He stayed with us for three years. When he came, he was thin and white; he was just about half-hungered to death. By the time he'd been with us for a month, he'd filled out and looked happy. You wouldn't have thought he was the same lad. At first I had to fix him up with coats and boots, he was that poor."

At Penrith, hirings were known as "termweek". Being hired here, as elsewhere, was the prelude to a week's holiday. "You left one place on Saturday, and went to the next place on the following Saturday." The farm man carried his possessions, such as a change of clothes, in a tin trunk. During the leanest times, it was enough for a man to have a place to sleep and eat. At Ulverston Hirings, "I heard a chap at one side o' t'street shout out: 'Hey, Bill, has ta got hired?' 'Aye—has thou?' 'Aye. I've got my feet under another fellow's table for six months. I'm all right!' "

A Borrowdale lad who began work at the age of 13 had been told by his schoolmaster: "You can go to work. We can't do any more for you here." He began work at Grange Farm at Martinmas, hiring for six months at £4.10s. Tommy Graham, the Keswick carter, collected his tin trunk on the next visit to Borrowdale, and it was delivered to Grange Farm. The sleeping quarters of the farm lad, above the kitchen, were approached by a ladder, and so constricted was the space beneath the slanting roof that he could not open his trunk unless he first slid it towards the bed. This bed was metal-framed, and a feather mattress was provided.

There was a skylight to admit light, though in winter the farm lad went to bed with a candle as illumination. Little time was spent in the bedroom, and at 6.30 a.m. in summer—earlier, if there was anything special—and 7 a.m. in winter, the farmer roused him with a shout. And so he went forth, wearing an old jacket, a shirt made by his mother—the shirt fastened at the back—corduroy trousers ordered from Mr Huggins, of Ambleside, who was a "bag man", and clogs made by Ernie Plaskett of Rosthwaite (they cost 10s). At that time, many farm men had sleeved waistcoats.

The plight of the servant girls who found themselves in the employ of unsympathetic farming families was a matter of local gossip, though fortunately most girls were well looked after. There was practically nothing else a girl could do on leaving school, but go into "service", and during several years of work, under the supervision of the farmers' wife, or the housekeeper of a large private home, she was taught a number of basic crafts.

Girls as well as boys attended the hirings. At Keswick, at about the time of the 1939-45 war, a servant girl could be employed for about 3s.6d. a week. The wage was paid at the end of the six months' term. A girl who stood the hirings at Ulverston accepted the shilling offered by a farming couple, "and I was stuck at their place for six months—for £6. I had to do everything about the house." Two girls who already had jobs "stood" at Penrith to "see how far anyone would go with wages." One of them who was offered £7 was receiving only £5.10s. at the place where she was already employed!

A servant girl in Mardale was hired when 14 years of age; she went to Chapel Hill, and managed to avoid attending the hirings, the position having been secured for her through the local vicar. She was living at Keld, and mother accompanied her to Chapel Hill. All her possessions were in a "canvas trunk". "I went out of Mardale only once during the six months' term. I never spent a penny except for collection at church on Sunday."

Large houses had many servants, for inexpensive labour was plentiful. A Langdale girl who found a job at White Craggs, Clappersgate, having been recommended for the work by the housemaid, was paid 5s a week and walked to her home for the half day which was the only break in the working routine. The servants were expected to attend church on Sunday. At Rydal Hall, where the le Flemings were well disposed towards their staff, a special celebration for them was planned at Christmas, when dancing took place in the servants' hall, to music provided by a local band.

A girl employed for farm work was paid "according to size and wit". A broad back was useful in the days when there was much heavy manual work. In Kentmere, "our servants mostly came from Barrow. They'd just left school, at 14 or 15, and were in effect serving their time, learning how to do household work. As they got older, they naturally got better wages, and then they got married. Some of 'em became farmers' wives." Also in Kentmere: "If you liked a servant lass, you'd say, as term came to an end, 'Are you stayin'?' She'd say: 'Yes'. If it was a lass who was brought up in the town, you'd know then that she'd never think of going back; she'd stay on the land."

In Mardale: "I started work at 5 a.m. and finished between 10.30 and 11 at night, for eightpence a day!" A Borrowdale man recalls: "I remember my mother saying that when she was a servant girl at High Lodore, she had to get up early in a morning and go out and wash in the trough. As mother was rushing about upstairs, having just got out of bed, Jane Wilson would shout: 'What's ta dewin', Laura?' 'Oh—I'se fastening me brat.' 'Nay—fasten it when thou's coming downstairs—and lowse it when thou's going to bed.'" At Seathwaite: "First the servant girl shook the mats, outside. Then she scrubbed the flags, and waited till they were dry before t'mats were put back. She did that every day, without fail."

In the days before piped water was a normal amenity, water was moved into the house in pails. At a farm in the Whitcham Valley, "we'd fetch all the water from t'beck." The water supply for Wilson Place, Little Langdale, was a well. "We had a sink in the kitchen, but no taps!" When the level of the water in the well dropped during a dry spell, an opportunity was taken to clean it out. By this time, the pail was being filled by a man who got down on his hands and knees so that he could reach the water." Water from hill streams was deliciously cold, a boon during a hot spell in summer, when soft butter was "stood" in it overnight. By morning, the butter was workable! "When I went down into Suffolk, early in the first world war, I wondered whatever was to do wi' t'watter. I never seemed to git a proper wash or proper shave. That water was off t'chalk, real hard!"

At Stool End, Great Langdale, "the kitchen had hooks in the ceiling. There were flagged floors—and a stone slopston' under the far window, with just a cold water tap. Cooking was at an old black range, and a table ran practically the length of one side of the kitchen... Before the water supply was improved at Wall End, water was carried up from the beck."

Monday was washing day, an operation performed manually and likely to reduce the women of the house to prostration. In Mardale, "we went outside the house, to the stick shed, where the set-pot stood. We got a dozen bucketfuls of water from a pump over the sink in the house. The fire was lit early. You were running late if you didn't have the clothes on the line before 8.30 in the summer. We had a dolly tub, dolly legs, a wooden mangle—and dolly blue. Oh, and there was a rubbing board. The best clothes went through three rinses." In Little Langdale: "Our set-pot took an hour to warm up. You had to have plenty of good dry sticks. Coal was ower-dear." Elsewhere: "Anything went under the set-pot—we burnt all our rubbish, paper and things."

14

Sandwick
—on the shores of Ullswater

A typical farm kitchen was slate-flagged. There might be a "prodded" hearth rug. "We cleaned our flags with carbolic soap and water, though some people rubbed them with 'blue' to make them darker." Honister slate formed many a floor in Buttermere, and because "the dirt didn't get into it" the flags were easy to wash. "Certain areas were washed every day; the whole lot had a good scrub at the week-end." There was pride in keeping the flags clean. "When we were at Birk How, a chap came to buy a calf. He said: "I'll tell thee what, missus, your floor's a credit to you!' It did look nice, I must admit. We cleaned flags wi' soft soap from a tin—and plenty o' watter. We got down on hands and knees and scrubbed them flags."

In Borrowdale, "my mother pushed me in a pram from Seatoller to Grange; she washed at a house there. It was nine miles, there and back. Then she left me with fadder when he returned from work in the evening, and she'd go over to another house to do the ironing. She got a bob a day for washing, and same for ironing!"

The walls of many a Lakeland kitchen were lime-washed. A Little Langdale farmer went with a horse and cart to Coniston station to collect lime, and "we slak'd our own." The lime-washing was done twice a year, "especially round t'fireplace, where it got so dirty." At this farm, the ceiling was papered, for there was an old loft above it. Flecks of dirt would otherwise fall on the table. "The oak beams were papered as well." Wallpaper was ordered from the Co-op at Chapel Stile. "They sent the book round, and you picked what you wanted. That book went from house to house. In the 1930s, if you paid fourpence a roll for it, you thought it was a big price."

The living kitchen held a substantial fireplace, flanked by oven and boiler. The necessity for having a regular supply of hot water meant that the kitchen fire was usually roaring throughout the year. At Seathwaite: "We lit the fire with larch chats, then some kindling sticks, then coal. My uncles went to Keswick about once a month with a cart, sometimes two carts, and got coal from the station. It was a day's work." A Langdale farmer's wife, visiting Ambleside just before the 1939-45 war, met "a fellow who had come all the way from Durham with a wagonload of coal. He said: 'Where can I get rid o' this?' I said: 'Follow me—we'll have it off you.' He followed me to Side House, and I think I gave him £6 for the lot. He couldn't have been paid with that. He didn't come any more, though. He must have been called up when war broke out."

At Millbeck, Great Langdale, "I remember we black-leaded the fireplace once a week. The boiler had a tap; we used a ladin can to draw water. There'd be a coffee pot on the ledge above the oven, and some days hankies were laid across the open oven door to dry. We had a clothes rack, screwed to t'ceiling near that fire;

there were always clothes on it; they'd been put to 'air'." In Mardale, "we black-leaded t'grate, and mixed black lead wi' a drop of meths, so it would go further. Coal came from Shap station. I remember the steel-top fender, which we'd to burnish wi' polish and a bit of ash, sometimes powdered brick. Where t'boiler was, we put a bit o' paper on t'fender, or it would spot and rust." At Seathwaite, "there was a big box o' black lead (plumbago, from the local mine) we used to polish t'grates."

The Lakeland besom had a relatively short shaft—some three feet of ash—and a head made of birch "chat" gathered locally. The best "chat" was found on the mosses. Other besoms were made of ling, also broom—hence the alternative name for a sweeping brush. A well-seasoned besom lasted a long time if it was kept dry; a damp besom was quickly attached by fungus. The carpeting of house floors, and the use of vacuum cleaners, reduced the demand for the old product.

The centrepiece of a Lakeland living kitchen was a large table, which was regularly scrubbed. In West Cumbria, "mother got up at a quarter to five every morning t'sun ever shone. First job was to make a cup o' tea for everybody else, and then she'd put breakfast things out on t'big table. There were eight of us in the family. We'd all to find a place round yon table. It was a big 'un, though, and kept snowy-white wi' scrubbin'." In Little Langdale, "we had an old laundry table. Father sat at one end in his armchair—rush-seat, chintz cover—and mother was at other end on a 'copy', which had four legs. Rest of us sat on forms."

At Birk How, "a big shelf went right across the room, just below the ceiling. Here we put tins of biscuits, box o' tea, soap, tin o' buttons—owt that had to be handy." Another kitchen held an armchair, a rocking chair and "two or three hard chairs". A Great Langdale resident recalls "t'owd oil lamp and cannels. When we got 'lectric, we did miss the oil lamps. It's amazing the heat they put out, especially those Aladdins."

There might be a working kitchen, where particularly messy tasks were carried out. At Birk How, "back kitchen had a bin with feeding stuffs, a mangle, a table with a dish on it—we used it for washing up—and also the dolly tub, dolly legs and mangle. At Seathwaite, "your toilet was away across the yard. They used to clean it out now and again and spread stuff on t'land."

The better room, or parlour, "was only used for State occasions —weddings, funerals and the like. There was all the better furniture here. Ours had a round table with a coloured cloth, rocking chair and 'easy' chairs with antimacassers. There were plenty of ornaments and pictures. If anyone had a piano, it was usually cluttered up with photographs." In Kentmere: "Parlour? I was never hardly in it." Wall End, Great Langdale, had a floor covered by "a crowd of skin mats." In the period before the 1914-18 war,

17

a good many sheep were killed and the mutton supplied to local households. The cured sheepskins were spread about the house. "When things got better, after the war, the potters started coming again, buying our skins." At Birk How: "It was supposed to be a sitting room, but it had only a flagged floor and an iron grate, with not much furniture. Some people called it a parlour. We always falled it 'front end'. It was draughty and cold."

Bedrooms could be cheerless places. In Mardale, "there was a wooden floor, iron bedsteads with brass knobs, feather mattresses ... We usually washed downstairs, in the kitchen, but visitors had a jug full of water, in a basin, on the dressing table in the bedroom." A hired man in the same district slept on a "caff" (chaff) bed, the material with which it was packed having been collected on threshing days. In Langdale: "My mother-in-law helped me to make a feather bed when I was first married. We got a new 'ticking', dressed the feathers. You had to cut the ends off the quills, or even strip 'em off by hand if they were big. We also made some feather pillows." In Little Langdale: "Our bed had a straw mattress, with a feather mattress on top.

A Little Langdale bedroom was "open to t'top"—there was no under-drawing—and the sleepers were exposed to the worst of the weather. "It used to snow ontil us when we were in bed...We looked up to slates and rafters. Auntie Mary used to have a big four-poster bed, with curtains round, but ours was an open bed. Before I was married, I was lying on that bed one winter neet when it began to snow. I could feel t'snow. I pulled clothes over me and went to sleep. Next morning, I had to carry swillsful o' snow downstairs." In the Whitcham Valley: "They say you never die in a feather bed, but you do!"

Quilting in winter was a regular occupation in Kentmere. "My grandmother made some lovely patchwork quilts; she cut out patterns, squares or diamonds. I was going to school at the time, and every dinnertime, when I came home, there was a 'cushion' full of needles. I had to thread them, because granny's eyesight was not very good."

What They Ate

IT WAS "PODDISH" for breakfast—thick porridge, made in a pan over an open fire, stirred with a stick called a thible, and served in basins. It was vital for the diner to clean up the basin, for that same vessel was used for a drink of tea! At Skelwith Bridge, "they set t'pan in t'middle o' table, and you could help yourself." In Borrowdale, "we had a round table, with one big shank."

Some farmers grew oats and took them to the local miller. In Upper Lunesdale: "They grew it, brought it, we handled it, and then they took it away!" The miller also sold oatmeal to the cottagers, one of whom might wander down to the mill for a couple of stone. "He'd sling it across his back and walk away." In Great Langdale, "we got our oatmeal from the Windermere grocers; they sent a chap round for orders, once a month, and stuff was delivered a day or two afterwards. You could buy oatmeal that was medium, fine or pinhead. I like pinhead the best; it made lovely porridge."

In Borrowdale, "they put a bowl of milk on the table. There was a ladle in it. You could have as much of this milk on your porridge as you wanted." Not everyone was thrilled by porridge. In West Cumbria: "I was nivver sorry when we gev over 'aving it! When you had a basin of porridge, you wanted damned all else! Porridge only lasted you about an hour, at t'outside, and you were soon hungry again. Course, in those days, lads were always hungry!" A farm man who had a "poor spot" related that whenever he returned to the farm he could smell burning porridge. "As soon as t'farmer saw me coming, he stuck a pan of old porridge on the fire and heated it up for me supper. I was sick of porridge, bread and cheese!" At Seathwaite, "we had porridge at night."

For breakfast, the porridge was usually supplemented by bacon and egg. In Kentmere, "generally you always got an egg, even if you didn't have any bacon." At a farm in Great Langdale, "it was porridge and a bit o' bacon' Sometimes a drop or two o' syrup was put on the porridge." Eggs were usually to be seen but not eaten at a farm in the Whitcham Valley. "We didn't get many eggs,

I'll tell you. Mother used to sell those!"

Oatmeal was prepared as porridge or oatcake. In Upper Lunesdale, "nearly everyone made oatcake; they used backstones, and the thinner you could make it the better. There was nothing better than oatcake with a bit o' decent butter on it." In Great Langdale, "we made ours in the oven, cut into squares, put in a baking tray. It had to be thin. You can make a meal off haverbread and a nice bit o' cheese. Course, you always had to have plenty of butter on it." The true haverbread was long and thin, made on a backstone and hung up to dry, where the pieces resembled wash-leathers. "They used to come round Kendal selling that sort." At Wilson Place, Little Langdale, "there was a big backstone in the kitchen, and you put brackens underneath when you wanted to bake oatcakes on top. It was simple stuff to make: oatmeal, fat and water, with a bit o' salt. It had to be rolled out thin. When it was baked, you broke it into pieces and put it in a basket to 'keep it'."

Food on a dales farm was plain but adequate. For "ten o' clocks" in the field, there might be coffee from a blue enamel can, and bread and cheese. In Borrowdale, "we sometimes got a big lump of gingerbread. The coffee came in 'tin bottles', and at ploughing time we hung the bottles on the horses' hames till we needed a drink." Near Coniston, "coffee time at our place was nine o' clock. We'd had our breakfast about seven!" Some farmers spurned coffee or even tea; "they generally had a pint o' water after a meal." In Great Langdale, the mid-morning "bait" consisted of "anything that was going—bread and syrup, a sandwich or two or a bit of pasty." At Skelwith Bridge, "coffee pot was emptied once a week, and egg shells popped in to clean it."

The break at noon for "dinner" was also an opportunity to feed and rest the horses, if ploughing or haymaking was being undertaken. "Hosses had a full hour; the farm man was expected to eat and drink quickly, and then do work about the buildings." In Borrowdale, "the mid-day feed was usually roast meat, with rice pudding or 'dumpling' (boiled pudding)." Of a farm at Skelwith Bridge it is recalled: "There were always plenty o' taties and some milk. There were no *cooks* in those days. Farmers' wives were the worst cooks in the world. They'd get a great lump of meat, boil it for Sunday, and we'd have it cold for t'rest of that week."

In the Whitcham Valley, "mother had a big old-fashioned cooking pot with three legs. She'd put a plucked hen in it, and all the vegetables, and that would make a real good dinner for us when we came home from school." Tatie pot was everybody's favourite dinner. "You got your meat, and put it in a big tin with onions, salt and pepper, then put taties on top." In Little Langdale, it was called tatie hash. "They call it Irish stew today. You diced the meat and put it in with water and carrots and turnips, brought it to the boil and kept it boiling a while. Then you put your potatoes on in lumps, and they mashed therselves while it was cooking. About half an hour before dinner-time, you might put some black puddings on top. Main job was to get it well warmed through.''

There is some confusion between a tatie pot and a hot pot, which may be the same basic dish with minor variations in different areas. In Langdale, "a hot pot has same ingredients as a tatie pot, but it's drier. It's done in the oven, not in a pan.'' The hot pot has for long been a feature of social gatherings, such as hunt suppers. In West Cumbria, hot pot consists of "mutton and potatoes, black pudding, onions and sich like....'' Most of the ingredients were of local origin. In the Whitcham Valley, "father grew everything—potatoes, cabbages, carrots, even celery.'' At Bampton, "the main meal was usually a meat course—stew and dumplings. At Chapel Hill, we butched our own sheep and pigs.'' In Upper Lunesdale, "there were always plenty o' rabbits, and you could poach salmon out o' t'beck. There'd be a pheasant now and again, and maybe a partridge or two!''

The mid-day meal included substantial puddings: rice, sago and a variety of steamed creations. In Mardale, each autumn, "we had blackberry dumplings. We'd line a basin with pastry, blackberry and sliced apple, then lay some pastry on top. It was covered with a cloth and steamed.'' Great Langdale housewives sometimes produced sago pudding, "but nobody seemed to care a lot for it... We used to have a lot of Spotted Dicks—dumpling with currants in it, and a nice sauce. Before Bird's Custard came out—and the first time I tasted it I'd be 10 or 11 years old—mother usually made a paste flour with milk and then poured boiling water on to it. She often added a lump of butter and some sugar. It made quite a good sauce. At Christmas-time, there'd be a bit of the short, hard stuff in it!''

Tea was an insignificant meal. At Skelwith Bridge, "there'd be oatcake and slices of white bread. Pastry didn't come along very frequently.'' A Borrowdale farm gave tea "a miss''. Tea at a farm in Great Langdale consisted of "bread and butter, jam and cheese, cakes and pasties.'' In Mardale, "we had bread and butter and jam. There was home-made cake, but not much of that.''

A large number of Lakeland farmhouses served "afternoon teas''. It was said of Chapel House in Borrowdale that this was the only farm in the valley where visitors were not catered for. A special treat for a girl at Seathwaite was a trip by horse and trap to Keswick on a Saturday to sample a sixpenny meal at a cafe. That meal consisted of a hot pie, cup of tea and two slices of buttered bread. Meanwhile, at Seathwaite, more substantial teas were offered to visitors at 1s. 4d. There was a pot of tea, both brown and white bread, scones, jam and rum butter and "three sorts of cake." Visitors to the *Dungeon Ghyll* hotels, in Langdale, sampled lemon cheese, made in winter and kept in large pots, the tops of which were covered with paper that had been soaked in whisky, to keep the contents fresh. At the *Dun Bull*, Mardale, ham and eggs were prepared in a huge cast iron frying pan.

Supper on a dale farm began at 6 p.m. or 6.30 p.m. In Borrowdale, duck eggs frequently appeared on the table, for the farmer kept a moderate number of ducks. Cold meat was another popular item. At Threlkeld Hall, a farm man, on finishing work for the day, was offered a pint of beer (at haytime, it was "a pint of beer for every cartload of hay delivered after six o' clock").

Christmas Day saw the various meals run into each other. At Grange Farm, Borrowdale, breakfast was augmented and for the mid-day meal the diners tucked in to goose. Cumberland sweet pie was made from fat mutton—"as fat as you could get"—plus currants and raisins, sultanas, peel and brown sugar. "They put it in a dish, with a crust on it, and it was sweet—too rich for me; I couldn't do with it. You warmed it up everytime you wanted it. The more often you warmed it up, and the better it was. It got syrupy, and a dark colour." In Little Langdale, "brandy butter's not much, but rum butter is grand; we often made some up for Christmas." Such butter was presented in a butter bowl, "a little round bowl with a lid on."

Sheep were at the centre of Lakeland economy. Years ago, the farmers would kill off many old wethers, and the flesh was dried, just like the ham of a pig. In Little Langdale, "we used to think that a three year old gelt ewe was the best mutton there was. When I was at home, in the bad years (1930s), I used to go round getting orders for wethers. We didn't bother to take 'em to Broughton mart or Ambleside fair, because it wasn't worth it. When the orders were in, fadder and me would set on and maybe kill two or three sheep in a week. He would stick 'em and I would skin 'em. We cured the legs. It would be getting on for a fortnight before the meat was ready. We hung the meat up in the 'beef baulk' (loft) above the fire. Cured mutton had a flavour of its own."

At Birk How, in the same valley, "we used to dry mutton in that big chimney. We chose thick part o' t'shoulder an' t'legs'. Put salt and salt petre on 'em for about a week. Sheep's head was used for broth. I loved brains—sheep brains, pig brains; I'd eat any. I used to skin 'em, split 'em, take brains out and wash them well to make a thick broth. Butchers nearly always gave sheep heads away." If a sheep head was on the small size, "we whanged it into t'dog hut."

A Langdale man hawked fresh mutton around Elterwater and Chapel Stile, charging 6d a pound. "Salted leg dangled from the beams of the kitchen. You put a little bit of salt petre on the bone end, and salt on the flesh. We lived a good deal on hot pots and tatie hashes in those days." A former shepherd says: "I don't like mutton. I've seen that many wicks in it!"

Almost every family kept a pig or two, "butched" it in the back-end of the year and cured it for winter consumption. At Sawrey, "biggest pig I butched weighed 30 stone. It had been reared down at Cunsey." Those were the days before humane methods of slaughter. At Troutbeck, "I was dared to butch a pig. It was a little dark 'un, going off its legs. Chap I was with said: 'Bet thou daren't tackle it.' I said: 'There's nobody dare me.' I butched the pig—and I got the job ever after..." The farmer at Seathwaite, in Borrowdale, kept two or three pigs. "I remember the great excitement when it was pig-killing time. That was in the days when they used a blocker (mallet) to stun a pig before it was stuck. Us kiddies used to be watching. Then, if the pig didn't drop first bat, we'd be off to tell grandfather he'd had two shots at it!" The "blocking" was carried out when the pig was standing, "and then it was just thrown on to t'creel. We sometimes got an old fellow called George Bennett to come and do the two pigs together."

Pig-killing was a job for the colder weather, and—according to a man in Great Langdale—"the real old-timers wouldn't kill a pig till it had eaten a bag of oatmeal, 16 stone. You finished a pig off with oatmeal, and that's where the good flavour came from. We used to make oatmeal balls, or some good porridge, and fed it to the pig... The men helping with pig-killing got mulled ale: boiled beer with brown sugar and ginger, served piping hot. On a really cold day, it warmed 'em up." In Mardale, "we gave small potatoes to the pigs; it was called crowdie. When we'd put the potatoes in the trough, we put some 'blue' (skimmed) milk with it." A Kent-mere man remembers when the sow was taken to the boar, a distance of 10 or 12 miles. "We put the sow in a cart which had the shelvings on and a sheet over the top.... Most of the piglets were sold off when they got to 14 weeks old."

In Great Langdale: "While the pig was being killed, someone had to stir the blood all the time or it would curdle. We had an old porridge stick, with two prongs. If the blood was beginning to go awkward, you forgot about the stick and put your hand in, with the fingers spread out... As soon as the pig was dead, you put the basin of blood in front of the fire to keep warm till you could make black puddings." For this delicacy, boiled barley was added, and "when you'd boiled the puddings, you put them on to brackens or straw till they went cool. I never inquired why they used brackens. Black puddings were usually made on the day the pig was killed, and next day you'd set off preparing sausage meat. I remember dad putting a stick over two hooks in the farm kitchen, and draping black puddings over the stick."

The pig was usually killed on a creel. "Then you had to scrape the outside, using warm water and a clean white cloth. You washed it down and took it to the barn, where you shaved it and opened it up. The shaving was done with a Sheffield knife which had an edge like a razor. A man could pluck a hair from his head and cut it with the knife. That's how sharp it was. You had to do your job reet, or they were on to you like a ton o' bricks.'' The pig was hung up and left for a day; then it was cut up.

Dales farmers could not resist the sporting aspects of Lakeland life. ''Once, they were going to kill a pig at Stool End. Mrs Martindale got the boiler boiling. Everything was ready. Jim Mitchell and my father went to catch the pig. Old William was waiting with a bucket to catch and stir the blood. ''They were just going to put the pig on the stool when the hounds came through. They let the pig go, and went off with the hounds. The fox was caught under the waterfall at Dungeon Ghyll, Margaret, the Martindale's daughter, had a terrier which wasn't much good. William picked it up, rammed it under his arm, and coming back from the hunt he said: 'We'll have to tell Margaret that Jippy worried yan fox.' He added: 'It nivver went near it!' The pig lived until Monday.''

To make black puddings or sausages it was necessary to clean some of the intestines of the pig. ''They were easy to turn yance you got a start, especially if you were working under a tap. Once you got a start, you just held 'em under a tap and it just runs through as easy as can be.'' Of Cumberland sausage, a butcher relates: ''You can fry it, cook it in the oven, eat it hot or cold— and it's full of meat... Cleaning intestines was a messy job because they were turned inside out. New starters to the trade got 'em ready, and more experienced men did the scraping.''

The man who cut up the pig secured two hams, two shoulders, two flitches and the head. In Great Langdale, ''we ate everything— except squeal. Apart from the head, the snout could be boiled, ears were put into t'brawn, and the tail helped to make a good broth.'' Pig cheek was a delicacy. Near Coniston, ''some of those blooming great Cumberland pigs—about 40 stone weight—had blinking cheeks like lile hams.'' Pig foot pie appeared on the table each autumn. ''Our mother would scald and clean t'trotters—they boiled down to a jelly—and put some black pudding in, with a crust on top.'' In Little Langdale, ''I never cared for it, but my uncles were daft on it. Jelly, bones and bits o' meat—it was far too greasy for me!''

The major parts of the pig received special attention. In Kentmere, ''we did flitches flat, putting 'em on a table on a clean white cloth. There'd be a frying pan full of salt on the fire, and that salt was hot and dry. Another bowl had cold salt and salt petre. You laid it on the table, got hot salt and spread it on meat about a quarter of an inch thick and started to rub it. You rubbed till the pig side sweated, and then you'd done enough. You turned it over, and got hot salt and sprinkled it all over, putting a little gentle touch of sugar, and then cold salt on top. On top o' that went the salt petre, and you didn't want much. It had to be handled gently. You didn't want it to dry out too fast, and it had to have the right taste. Then you did your hams and shoulders, working salt petre into the ends of the bones. We put pig meat on the stone slabs where we usually had milk things. When it was ready, you washed the meat down and hung it up to dry."

A dales farm kept two or three geese and a gander. "They were a jolly good guard. If anyone stirred of a neet-time, you'd hear t'geese shout." Each December, the flock—by then augmented by 30 or 40 young of the year—was severely culled for the Christmas trade. A goose was plucked, bled (the blood being used for black puddings) and plucked. "A goose has a top coat and waistcoat; it has to be plucked twice!" In Great Langdale: "It's nowt pulling feathers out, but thee try pulling the blessed down." Goose grease was "grand for bronchial trouble. You really can't beat it for your chest. Nobody bothers in these days." In Mardale: "Fell lads greased their boots wi' it, and it went through t'uppers on to their socks."

Goose wings were kept for spring-cleaning, being used to reach cobwebs that had formed behind large pieces of furniture. In Buttermere: "I used goose wings for knocking down cobwebs in t'outbuildings." Goose feathers were used for mattresses and pillows. "We had a big set-pot, and mother put goose feathers in it to dry 'em off, before stuffing 'em into a feather bed."

Baking day flavoured the entire house with wholesome scents. In Langdale, "mother started early in the morning. She was starting to knead bread when we set off for school at a quarter to eight." In Mardale, "we made all our own bread, a stone at a time. A stone of flour made eight loaves. We baked for the week, keeping the bread in a big pot. The bread kept fairly well." At the head of Great Langdale: "We baked our own bread and cakes. The grocer came once a month. When we were going to school, we'd bring up the yeast for Mrs Martindale (Stool End Farm) and mother, and at holiday-times the postman obliged. He would bring anything else if you asked him."

Grocers delivered goods in Kentmere, including 10 stone bags of flour for bread-making. "Those bags used to stand in the pantry." Dales housewives had their favourite recipes which were made regularly. From the oven came scones and gingerbread, currant and apple pasties, with rhubarb pasty in season. In Borrowdale, "grandfather wouldn't have a fruit cake at Christmas; he liked something plain, and so grandmother made some, with those great big raisins in it. She flavoured that cake with rum."

At most farms, sweets were rarely seen, but toffee was a "regular rarity". It was often made to be eaten at the festivities on November 5. "Sometimes two or three farming families met at one farmhouse for a Toffee Join. The ingredients of the toffee were: 1 lb treacle: 1 lb farm butter; 1 lb brown sugar; a tablespoonful of vinegar and one of cold water. The toffee was boiled in an iron pan over the fire, and it was tested in cold water. When cool enough to be handled, it was twisted—with buttered hands—into lengths about one inch and a half thick and four or five inches long. Some people liked it rolled in oatmeal. It was just lovely to suck and crunch."

A Kentmere man who delivered a calf to a farm in Longsleddale was invited to sit down so that he could retail the local gossip. The family was just sitting down to dinner, but he was not invited to join the feast. "Owt fresh ower Kentmer?" asked the farmer. "Aye," said the farm man. "Pig ferrid and brought forth 14 piglets, but yon old sow nobbut has 13 paps." "Why, mi lad, what's t'odd 'un bahn ter hev to do?" asked the farmer, to which the farm man replied: "Same as me: I doubt it'll have to sit back!"

About Herdwicks

THERE'S A LOT of "sad grund"—crag, bracken, bog—on the fells. "The Herdwick is the only breed of sheep that does well up there. Many a time I've wondered how they manage to stick the weather. My farm (in upper Langdale) doesn't get any sun for weeks on end in winter. When there's no sun, the snow and frost can't thaw off. Sheep have a bad time." Herdwicks are nearly as thrifty as deer. In Borrowdale, through the winter, "sheep live on moss and crag ends, little bits o' briar and bits o' shoots."

Hardiness is one of the Herdwick's outstanding qualities. "A Herdwick can live and thrive on the scantiest herbage of the most rugged mountains. I've known a sheep be covered by snow for 21 days—and recover." In Longsleddale, "nine times out of ten, sheep come down the fell before they can be trapped by drifts of snow, and only odd ones are overblown. Tom Fishwick found one of our ewes that had been under snow for three weeks. He had seen a fox sitting on the snow, watching something that was out of sight. Tom went across to have a look and found the sheep. We put it in the barn, and gave it new milk morning and night for three weeks. It went on champion." Another sheep which spent a long time under snow desperately chewed its wool to keep alive.

In Little Langdale, "we dug three sheep out after they had been in snow for three week. Foxie had found 'em. It scratted in, and chewed the leg of a sheep that had died. There was yan of ours in that drift, and it was still alive. It was quite bright when we got it out, though it had eaten a lot o' wool off dead sheep ... When a blizzard comes, a sheep goes into a sheltered spot and turns its back round. Snow blows over it." Near Coniston, "some people try to tell you that a Herdwick will live where others will die. I don't think that's quite right. I seem to loss as many Herdwicks as I loss any other sort... One winter I lost over 300 ewes, and most of 'em would be Herdwicks. They're such stupid beggers. They won't start to eat until it's too late, and they let therselves get too low..."

The Herdwick strain of sheep has been on the fells for centuries. Animals form a real and lasting attachment for the native heaf and, in fact, for quite limited areas. In Great Langdale, "I bet that if we walked to a certain spot near here there'll be an old ewe, last year's lamb (hogg), and lamb of the year before (shearling). Lambs find their own mothers on the fell when they come back after spending a winter near the sea." Herdwicks suit the Lakeland fells. "You can't beat them. Sometimes one will get cragfast and we have to go down on ropes for it, and sometimes one or two break their necks on the crags, but the number of accidents is quite small really." In Borrowdale: "They've been bred on these hills for ages. Hardiness has matured in them." There have been subtle changes as a result of selective breeding. "Fleeces used to be longer. They likely got a bit taggled in snow, but they seemed to cope."

In the days of inexpensive labour, a farmer could afford to employ a shepherd, "though if it wasn't a very busy time, you did other work as well, especially through winter. Shepherding in these days isn't like what it was then. They can bung them away to the fell today, and they're finished till they want to bring them in to spain lambs. They bung 'em back again, and bring them in to dip." The old shepherds knew every inch of the terrain, and ensured an even distribution of sheep. "I once went round back of Langdale Pikes three times in a single day—twice while shepherding and once at night. Someone asked me to help carry down a visitor who'd injured himself." At Grange Farm, Borrowdale: "We took hay to the sheep on the fell, which was unhandy, lying off the Langstrath Valley. We'd set off with a horse and cart load of hay, and store it in an outbuilding. We put some of the hay in large hessian sheets. You put your head between the knots and staggered up the fell."

Old-time shepherds going to the fell made no special preparations. A man simply picked up a stick, called for a dog or two, and strode off. "I'd appen have a sandwich or two to eat. If I didn't feel hungry, I gave t'sandwiches to t'dog. I had a 'blow out' at night. A shepherd at Troutbeck had "four and a quarter miles to walk from stable door to t'fell gate. If it was hot weather, you wanted to be away between four and six o'clock." In Little Langdale, "if you were showing sheep, like we used to do, they could be quiet. They would come to you, because you handled 'em a lot. Out on t'fell, they were independent, and wily. If they didn't want to be gathered in they'd skulk away at back of a crag, out o' t'road, and once they did this, they'd try it again."

A Seathwaite farmer "never got lost on t'fell, but we once had a lad that did, and he slept out all night. Mist came down, and he crept under a stone—him and t'owd dog; they cuddled up together. When mother got up next morning, lad and dog were coming across field as large as life!" In the 1914-18 war, when there was a shortage of labour on the farms, women quite often found themselves helping out with the shepherding. "I had to go to t'fell like a lad...I started when I was about ten, and I had my own dog when I was 12. Dad and I would set off in t'morning—and get back

sometime.''

A Great Langdale farmer was never lost, ''but yance I did get out of my latitude in a thick mist. I wanted to get to Red Tarn, and I said to missen: 'Thoo's takken t'wrang trod.' So I sat down and git my pipe out, and had a smoke, and while I were having a smoke, mist just split, and I was looking reet at Scawfell.'' Another local farmer, delayed on an excursion to the fell, ''landed down'' at Stool End at 10 p.m. ''Jim Mitchell was just looking round his stock before he went to bed. He said: 'Where hev you fella's come frae?' I said: 'We've just come down from t'top o' Bowf'l'.''

The maggot fly was a major summertime pest. At Troutbeck: ''In real hot, sultry weather you had to keep going, day after day, if you had a big expanse o' land. The fly worried sheep directly. Bluebottle laid its eggs on t'shoulder, if they were among brackens, but generally at back 'end. If there was a bit o' dirt on them at all, flies struck. You could always tell when a sheep had 'wicks'. It rubbed and skulked.''

A parasite lodging in the head of a sheep led to a condition known as ''sturdy''. ''You'd feel over t'head for a soft spot. Then heat an iron in t'fire, and burn through skull nice and quietly; you hadn't to press that hard on it. Then if you were right on t'sturdy, it used to come out through this hole. It was like a little bladder. You'd patch up t'poor old sheep with some pitch and a lile bit o' cloth. Pitch kept t'water out. Some sheep got better; some didn't.'' In Langdale: ''If we had a 'sturdy' sheep, and it had any meat on it, we used to eat it!''

A Troutbeck farmer ''yance took sturdy out of a Herdwick shearling. I asked blacksmith to mak me summat to cut through t'skull. You get a feather—quite a fluffy feather, not very strong— and feel where 'sturdy' is. There's a soft place i' top o' t'head, either one side or t'other; generally on opposite side to that sheep was walking round. If it were going round clockwise, well it'd be on t'opposite side. You burnt a hole in. I got a thing o' purpose, a little iron. You lifted loose bit o' skull out wi' a knife, then gently took out t'sac, with its eggs, using t'feather. You just put the feather in, and twisted it round gently till you got hold of it; then drew it out quietly. You sealed up the wound with a cloth, putting a bit o' pitch round t'edge o' cloth so the air couldn't get into it.''

Any stray sheep which a farmer and his men collected during a ''gather'' were returned to their rightful owners at a Shepherd's Meet, which in some cases was also an excuse for drinking and revelry. At *Dungeon Ghyll* , Langdale, ''it was mostly just a get-together for the shepherds of Langdale and Borrowdale. Then it developed into a sheep show and sports. It was held on the first Saturday in December, at the Old Hotel one year and the New Hotel in the following year.'' At Matterdale there was ''a fox hunt in the morning—and a good sing at night.'' In Langdale, ''a lot of men sang songs and got drunk and forgot to take the sheep home with them. One man took his brother's dog, got drunk—and sold the dog!"

One of the most famous Meets took pace at the *Dun Bull*, Mardale, now covered by the water of a reservoir. The event took place on the Saturday nearest November 20. "Afterwards there was clay-pigeon shooting and hound trailing. Everything in the main rooms had to be hidden away except the chairs. Beer was distributed in buckets. Folk came for the day, but it might be 10 days before the last of them left the inn." The value of the Meet declined when telephones became common, for farmers with stray sheep could then ring up the owners and arrange for their collection.

The sheep farmer's calender usually began in autumn, when he went to the fairs at Keswick and Eskdale and hired rams, which are also known as tups or tips. New tups were needed for a "change of blood". The best were "spokken for" in advance. A number of farms were visited by flockmasters in advance of the fairs, and such a day out became known as Tip Sunday. "West Head at Thirlmere would have a 'Sunday'. So would Glencoyne, Seathwaite, Gatesgarth. Farmers turned up in time for t'dinner, and at Seathwaite we'd summat roasted, maybe a couple o' legs o'mutton; also a great big rice pudding wi' raisins in it. There was apple or currant pasty. And glasses o' whisky."'

Tups presented for the hirings were adorned with red colouring to make them look more distinguished. In Little Langdale, "we used to go to Red Tarn for our 'red', but it was a bad-coloured red. Dull. I used to carry it down a bag at a time." Eskdale (Esh'dl) Show was noted for its tups. "I've seen 70 or 80 tups being driven either to or from that show. Auld Isaac Thompson, of West Head, Thirlmere, took a week over t'job. They would fetch their tups to Grasmere, and then walk 'em into Little Langdale. Next day they'd take 'em over t'passes to Esh'dl, and on Friday they were at t'show—it was held on a Friday then. Next day, they'd drive more tups back to West Head." A Little Langdale farmer who walked tups to Eskdale—"it were seven miles from Fell Foot to Brother-ilkeld"—arranged to deliver the animals at about 10 a.m., and his father reckoned that the lad would be home again for milking at about 5.30. "You never seem to walk by yourself; there were plenty o' folk going to t'show."

A sheep farmer in Great Langdale "fetched tups from Eskd'l Show, some to Mardale and some to Longsleddale, also from Keswick. I did a fair bit o' droving at one time. We helped one another in those days, and I drove tups back for quite a few farmers. Tups were hired, of course. You could get a good tup for £1, but now they ask you a fairish price. Eskdale Show was always the last Saturday in September. Keswick Back End Fair was always on the first Saturday in October. Tups that had been hired were taken back to Eskdale for the first Friday in May, and to Keswick on the nearest Thursday to the 20th. And they had to be returned in good condition.'' A tup fair took place at Orton, in the east, being held on the second Friday in October. "Carts laden wi' tups set out from the fell districts the previous day. On Fair Day you could hardly get a horse into Orton..."

Broughton once had its tup-hiring fair, "but that died out a lot o' years ago. Tips used to be in t'street below t'owd *King's Head*. You got tips in October and took 'em back in May. Some folk used horses and traps, but tips were walked mostly. You couldn't do it now; you'd get run ower! It wasn't all that difficult to drive a tip, not if you'd a good dog. T'owd tips nearly knew where they were going: they certainly knew what they were going for!" A farmer in upper Kentmere bought his Rough Fell tips from Longsleddale, and often collected them from Jim Nicholson with a horse and cart." In Little Langdale: "I used to go to t'tip-hirings in t'back-end, but in May I'd send 'em back wi' somebody. I was always too busy lambing then." Tups being moved to Eskdale Show from Seathwaite, at the head of Borrowdale, went by way of Sty Head and were quartered overnight at Wasdale Head. In Buttermere, "some people would buy tips; others hired 'em. For Keswick Ram Fair, in the autumn, we travelled over the Hause into Newlands, then on to Keswick. But we used to hire one or two from Lanthwaite Green, and when the Nelsons were at Gatesgarth we always had one or two of theirs."

A Herdwick tup does not need to be told when it is mating time! "Tips start brekking out an' fighting. And *do* they fight! I've known 'em neck one another. You see 'em back a couple of hundred yards; they charge each other and come together with such clouts. You can hear t'crack o' skulls half way round t'parish." In Little Langdale, "I wouldn't like to have my hand between their heads when they meet. Herdwick tips often had gurt scars ower their eyes, though it wasn't often that a tip brok its neck. What we called 'mug tups'—Suffolks or Wensleydales; they were fancy bred 'uns—wouldn't stand much of a knock." Near Coniston: "There was a Herdwick tip, and when it came to a gate it put on a bit of a spurt. Aye. It went straight through'gate, and then walked on!" Rough Fell tups, in the south-east, engaged in memorable fights. "They knew t'time o' year. As soon as that time o' year comes, you'll see 'em wandering out. Sometimes you had to couple 'em together. They would fight till one gave in. Once, I saw a tup have its neck brokken ... A couple o' tups run back width of a field sometimes, then charge an' meet in t'middle. I've seen their hindends go up and nearly touch wi' t'force of collision."

Old-time Herdwick men sustained a custom which prevented young sheep from being mated. It was known as "clouting the

The Dalesman's Home

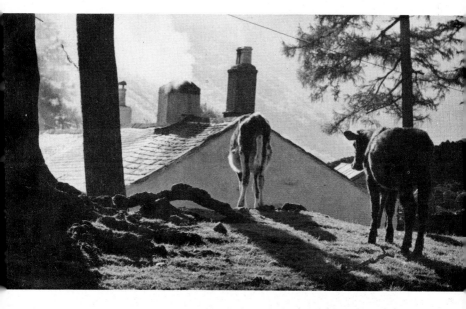

Above: Stonethwaite Farm, in Borrowdale.
Below: Farmhouse kitchen in Great Langdale.

A BORROWDALE SHEEP FARMER

John Richardson, of Seathwaite, with pony and Herdwick sheep.

THE HERDWICK MEN

Above: A trio at Eskdale Show — W. Wilson, of Bassenthwaite, W.M. Wilson, of Glencoin, Ullswater, and J. Richardson, of Buttermere. *Below:* A gathering to assess the quality of sheep.

A SOLITARY FARMSTEAD
Driving geese at Blea Tarn, Little Langdale.

A Dog's Life in Lakeland

Above: Assembly of dogs in the cobbled yard at Seathwaite, head of Borrowdale.

Below: A springtime gathering by the road to Skiddaw House in 1906.

DUNNEY BECK FARM, NEAR GRASMERE

The cattle are of the Shorthorn type.

A TIME FOR CLIPPING

Above: "Boon" clipping on a farm in Great Langdale.

Below: A farmer concentrates on clipping off the fleece using hand shears.

MOTHERS' MEETING, HILL TOP FARM, NEAR GRASMERE.

twinters." Shearlings which were not to be put to the ram because they were too young to rear a lamb had 'twinter clouts', or small cloths, placed at their rear quarters. These cloths were taken off in spring to be washed and ironed for another season! They were made from old clothes or coarse sacking.

Scarcely anyone now living in Lakeland has first-hand experience of "salving", an operation which took place in the autumn, involving the "shedding" of wool and the application to the skin of a mixture of tar and grease. Salved sheep were said to winter best, and the tar was claimed to be effective against some sheep parasites. "They'd just finished with it when I became a servant, about start of t'first war, in Kentmere. They salved for pests, but it didn't do much good." In Newlands, "we did odd 'uns, using tar and a bit o' mutton fat. They did it in a shed they called 'salving house'." At Seathwaite: "My uncle used to tell of it; I knew how it was done." There was a salving house at Rosthwaite. "Edmond-sons, of Penrith, supplied the tar, and a farmer would buy a bit o' salving butter. Poor quality stuff. He might put a bit o' milk in t'salve to take sting out." Surviving for years at Birk How, Little Langdale, was the wooden bowl that held salve; the bowl had a long handle and was stuck into an appropriate part of the creel (on which sheep were salved or clipped).

At Bootle: "There was an old chap used to live beside us; he was ninety-summat when I would be in my teens (late 1930s) and he could remember salving. He said that stockings made out of wool that had been salved were far softer and lasted far longer, and you never got sore feet." Salving was in rapid decline in the upper Lune Valley before the 1914-18 war. "I was only a nipper lad, but remember that some farmers had great big pans and braziers for making t'salve. It looked like liquid bacon fat, and was brownly stuff. Somebody would put a sheep on the creel and tip it to one side. The wool just fell down. They parted wool, got some salve on their fingers and stroked t'skin. Then they pulled another lump o' wool over. It went on till they'd covered t'sheep."

Herdwick Billy recalled that the salve was made of Stockholm tar and Skinner grease, though very little tar was necessary. Sometimes the grease used was poor quality butter. "There were professional salvers. It was only possible for a man to salve from seven to 12 animals in a day. An average hill flock could not be salved in under three weeks. The work of these visiting salvers was checked by a "doctor" to ensure that the work had been done thoroughly. The sheds were counted by parting the wool down-wards. In Kentmere: "Father said it was a weary job. They must have been in a sticky mess by the time they'd done the whole flock."

Sheep-dipping replaced salving. "When they were to dip sheep at Seathwaite, two old men would chop wood for days on end and wheel it up in t'wheelbarrow to t'salving house. When you're dipping sheep, you should always dip at the same temperature as the day. They had a set-pot o' purpose at Seathwaite, and we heated up the water in it. Buckets of hot water from t'set-pot were poured into t'dipping tub.'' Insect pests were still troublesome. At Troutbeck, when a sheep had become badly infested with maggots "we clip't wool, poured Jeyes fluid on and that killed t'maggots. Then we rubbed sheep wi' whale oil to stop flies strikin' again.''

Hoggs (the young stock) went to wintering quarters in low country, often by the sea. In Little Langdale, "we walked 'em, in October, before tupping time. And, of course, we had to bring them back. Hogg Day was fifth of April, and you settled up with the farmers who'd kept 'em for you. I've paid as little as five bob.'' If sheep were to be wintered on the Solway flats, the operation might take a fortnight. Farmers and their men stayed the night at different farms en route: places which their families had patronised for many a year. Some 600 hoggs were walked from Seathwaite, at the head of Borrowdale, to Solway shore. In the autumn, the road down Buttermere-side had flocks of sheep, with about 100 in a flock. "Father sent his out Dissington way, through Lamplugh. He stayed overnight at Mockerkin, beyond Loweswater. It was quite a holiday for dad, really—the only time he got away from the farm overnight. Hoggs from Middle Fell, Langdale, were driven to Whitbarrow, and the first night of the journey was spent in the Windermere area. "We went to Whitbarrow to collect the sheep about March 25.''

Thrifty farmers gathered ash leaves at t'back end, keeping them in large sheets or kists and feeding them to the sheep in winter. At West End (Great Langdale): "My husband's grandfather carried ash leaves and hay, mixed, from Mill beck to a croft on the fellside; it was a place where they gathered sheep to sort them when they were at t'fell. Sometimes the leaves were carried in sacks on ponyback.''

At lambing time, a Langdale farmer's wife—not the farmer himself—tended the weakly or ailing lambs, which were kept in boxes near the kitchen fire. "Mother gave them cow's milk; she warmed it with a heated poker from the fire. The old drinking fellows used to warm up their beer in the same way.''

It was said of a good lamb that it should be cooked twice—yance on t'hill and yance in t'oven. At Wasdale Head, it was observed: "Sunshine is a great healer.'' At lambing time, a farmer going on his rounds with a companion on a cold, wet morning might comment: "It's a real tickler, isn't it?'' In such weather, it was vital for a lamb to take milk from the ewe as quickly as possible. Where difficulty was being experienced, a ewe was turned and firmly held. The lamb was placed in position to suck and then it was tickled at the tail root, stimulating it to drink. "The old routine was to git up at dayleet and go walk round them." At Troutbeck, "when you gathered in for lambing time, you usually had a few 'white lambs'—they've bin born on t'fell. If they survived at all they were good lambs; t'weaklings died off."

In Great Langdale: "My father would never let you touch a raven. He said they kept t'fells clean. "Them daup-crows (carrion crows) he would have shot. They're beggars wi' lambs. You don't get ravens doing it. Wicked owd devils is them daups."

About a fortnight before clipping time, fell streams were dammed with stones and soil (doors were used on occasion) and the sheep were given a thorough ducking. It cleaned the wool, and helped it to "rise". A 97-year-old observes: "I just mind washing time. We dammed t'beck, penned t'sheep up, then chucked 'em in." Sheep-washing took place under the railway viaduct at Beckfoot, by the upper Lune. "Howgill farmers nearly all washed their sheep up on t'fell. They used to sod t'beck up and run sheep through and poke at 'em wi' a big stick. It's surprising how it cleaned 'em." Near Bootle: "We washed yance or twice. You were supposed to get more per pound for your wool, but we never did. Anything you gained by washing, you lost in weight. You washed t'nature out of wool." Great Langdale: "Washing finished before my day. It faded because of t'maggots. Blowfly struck sheep before they were dry."

For the boon-clips, neighbours and friends gathered at a farm to shear the sheep. "Clipping time was never the same after t'first war." Fell Foot, Birk Howe and Base Brown were but three farms in the Langdales where sheep by the hundred and people by the score gathered on a special day to harvest the wool. "The men gathered before dayleet; they were ready on t'tops to gather the sheep when first light came.... For the clipping, they had two or three big strong lads catching sheep. We children used to take round bandages in case the sheep were cut. Another youngster would carry round the salve. Yet more children gathered up the wool. There were always a lot of short ends that had been clipped off. If they were clean, they were picked up and put in a heap. Folding fleeces was often left, to be a wet-day job. They just threw fleeces in a heap in the barn.

"Old Ikie Morris, from Pickles, the wool merchants of Kendal, was a dab-hand at folding fleeces; he often used to turn up at Middle Fell when I was a lad, and he was good to watch as he folded them up. In those days, they put handfuls of small clippings into a fleece before wrapping it. There was a knack in t'fleecing business... Women came round with the beer jug, and later there'd be tea, with sandwiches made of home-cured ham. When they had finished, at about six o'clock, they would sit down to a really good meal: a big hot pot. I remember that the men first washed outside, in shallow tubs. They stripped down to their

Gatesgarth—
near the foot
of Honister

waists. Some of the men, when they replaced their shirts, put on collars and ties for the meal and the dance that followed. A dozen, 20 or even 30 men sat down for the meal. There were terrible big do's at Troutbeck Park and Kentmere Hall. In Langdale, they used to dance in the barn. One of my uncles played his melodeon, and at about 4 a.m. he used to gently play *Now the Day is Over* as a sign that it was time everyone was getting home!''

All kinds of refreshments were served to the dancers—"tea and coffee, all sorts of cold drinks, all sorts of sandwiches, cakes and brandy snaps, filled with cream.'' Brandy snaps were served at Wall End. "When I was a little girl, I used to go across there when they were getting ready for their clipping, and in the front kitchen they had sticks spread out all over. When they'd baked the brandy snaps, they put them round the sticks to make them curl.'' The first world war killed the boon clip. "There were hardly any men left, and those that remained did the best they could...''

There was an old saying in the sheep country: "Keep shears and tips back.'' The tips, or tups, were kept back until late November, or even into December. Shears were kept back until late July. A ewe with a lamb was not in as forward a condition as other sheep. If the wool was removed too soon, the animal was clipped bare, starving the animal and the lamb, because the milk supply went. In the clipping season at Gillerthwaite, in Ennerdale, between 2,000 and 3,000 sheep were handled by over 20 shearers, who sat in a circle, being regaled with beer drawn from barrels. They were supplied with sheep by a small army of helpers. If anyone wanted a sheep at Gillerthwaite, they shouted "Billy Ben''. The first man who had supervised the catching and taking away of sheep was a shepherd of that name. He had been dead for many years, but was still remembered at clipping time.

A Herdwick has "roughish wool'' and is "hard to clip''. At Seathwaite, Borrowdale: "There were 1,102 sheep with the spot. We clipped hoggs first, then shearlings, then ewes. It went on for maybe a fortnight, even three weeks in some years. We used to have a 'fleecer' rolling up the fleeces. Years gone by, we wrapped wool in big sheets and took it by horse and cart to Keswick. In the year my father-in-law died, there were two lots o' clippings in store. Wool had been bringing twopence a pound, and he wouldn't sell. First world war broke out, and then they were wanting all the wool they could get. They paid a good price for it!'' Isaac Thompson, of West Head, Thirlmere, kept his wool clip for three years because it was bringing only threepence a pound. Eventually he had to sell it—for twopence.

At Kentmere Hall, a manufacturer of clipping machines, gave a demonstration in the yard on the day the usual helpers sat on the creels holding hand-shears. "They were interested and amused, for they did two sheep while the machine did one. They were comfortably seated; t'chap with machine was standing up getting back-ache." At Chapel Farm, Borrowdale, "there'd be six clipping, three catching, two smitting (marking). The catcher took away the fleece, lapped it up and it was thrown into a barn or other out-building. Then it was stacked in a big granary." In Mardale, when clipping began at the latter end of June or early July, "we clipped in the barn, if it was wet. Otherwise, we put the stools out in the yard. There'd be three or four clippers, with a couple o' lads catching, and another—usually an old man—folding up fleeces."

In Langdale, "there'd be perhaps a dozen helpers at Birk How, Sheep were gathered over a couple o' days. When I was a lad, I used to be t'doctor, an' carry t'sorve (salve) pot aboot, in case anybody nicked a sheep. It was bought-sorve; green was t'best." It is recalled that at Hart Head, Rydal, there might be 20 to 30 helpers. "They started a week or 10 days before haytime, and went to the various farms over a wide area, even in Patterdale."

A "boon clip" was held at Wall End, Great Langdale, but at Stool End "they didn't bother with one." Up to a dozen clippers were mustered at Wall End, and when Ezekiel Myers took over this Langdale farm in 1914, his father and two brothers came over from Seathwaite. "The owd chap sat in the middle of the yard, looking about to see how good or bad were the sheep turned over to father—they were very poor."

The boon-clip was a time of merriment and good feasting. At Kentmere Hall, in 1913, some 40 creels were arranged in the yard. "Everybody used to look forward to clipping day. You were well fed, and at t'finish up there was a big sit-down in t'barn. Trestle tables and forms were set out. Wives and servant lasses were there to help. It was a real 'knife and fork' do, with a big roast and trimmings, apple tart with cream. You could drink either beer or tea." At Rydal, "one of my first jobs in the morning was to pick a lot of gooseberries, and we made huge gooseberry tarts. There'd be beef, and a lump of ham put in the big pan and boiled. Everyone enjoyed the pease pudding that followed the main course."

The Clipping Party at Kentmere Hall actually took place in an outbuilding, and the wooden floor was smeared with candle fat. "I was never much of a dancer, but I used to enjoy listening to my old boss, Noble Gregg, as he played the melodeon. Dancing went on "till well into t'morning." Another who attended the Kentmere Hall party recalls the dancing—"they threw some stuff on to wooden floor to make it slape"—and also the sing songs. "There'd be dancing an' singing and occasionally t'beer can 'ud go round. At one 'do' a chap got tipsy, and they put him down the trapdoor they used for serving fodder to t'stock; he finished up in t'shippon down below."

The sheep stocks were "spained" about the middle of Sept-ember. Spaining was the act of separating the lambs from the ewes.

The draft ewes were taken to be sold, and many of the lambs would have their winter holiday at the coast and then take their place in the flocks on the fells.

Sheep farming was possible because, in the collie dog, the farmer had a means of quickly rounding up his stock. Many farmers and shepherds trained their own sheepdogs. At Troutbeck: "A dog trains itself really, as long as you keep on top of it. I had one that showed interest when it was six months old, but another dog was two years old before it did a stroke. Some folk used whistles when working dogs. Others just shouted. I used to whistle with my fingers, till these (false teeth) rather spoiled it." At Troutbeck Park, a farmer remembers "the old fell type of dog, a barker." Another man recalled "different kinds o' dogs; some were rough-haired, and others were clean and smooth-haired. I had both kinds. I liked a dog that'd bark, when you ask it to bark." In Great Langdale: "Best dogs work for one man only. I'd one, and if I let a pup out with it, it wouldn't work. Just sulked. You see, it was a good, stylish worker. Puppy made a mess o' things!"

Gap-walling was a regular job on a dale farm. In Great Langdale: "My father used to say to me, when I was little: 'Come on, you can pick lile stones up. You'll always be of some use." A Patterdale farmer allocated certain parts of the year to walling—"inside" walls before lambing time, "outside" walls afterwards. The stones used at Wasdale Head were of the rounded, beck-bottom variety. "If you could wall with Wasdale stone, you could wall anywhere." (Wordsworth compared the pattern of Wasdale walls to "a large piece of lawless patchwork"!) Most of the gaps appeared when there was a thaw after frosty weather. At the head of Eskdale: "When you saw a wall shutter in a hard spell, you knew it was going to thaw."

Cradle to the Grave

IN BORROWDALE, "our two weren't born bi' t'doctor. There was just the nurse. Before that, geyly often, it was just some old lady in the parish." Mrs Annie Nuttall used to help women in labour in the valley. "Lot's o' folk didn't bother about a doctor." Belle Thirwall, of Bothel, was another unqualified midwife who delivered scores of babies. "She arrived a day or so before the birth, and she looked after you for about a fortnight. She did all the work as well.

To be fair to the doctors of the time, who travelled through their vast practices on horseback, or with horse and trap, it should be noted that they did undertake many heroic journeys to attend to their patients. In Little Langdale, "they never told the doctor till three months before the time the baby was due." Dr Kendall, of Coniston, rode his horse "over to Black Hole and Cockley Beck." For a birth at Seathwaite, on Easter Sunday, 1906, "Dr Crawford came out from Keswick." When the birth was imminent, someone in the house made rum butter. "You always made a dish o' rum butter to offer anyone who came to see the baby. They made another dish when there was a christening." In Great Langdale, "everybody called to see the baby and was given bread with rum butter. It was usually rum butter. I like brandy butter myself!" The visitor would press a silver coin into the hand of the child. "I guess there'll be no one except me that does it now." The mother went to be "churched" before she visited another house.

Children living at remoter farms might walk two or three miles to attend school. "At Overend Farm, the highest in Kentmere, three children walked to school, and they never missed. One of those kids was only five years old." From a farm in the Whitcham Valley, "we used to go to school at Thwaite, nearly four miles away." At Wall End, Langdale, "we walked three and a-half miles each way, because school was at Chapel Stile. I started when I was six. If it was a real wet day, we didn't go to school."

Those who lived "unhandy" took provisions for the mid-day meal. In the Whitcham Valley, "mother used to make our tea in a tin container, and the schoolmaster put the tin on a little stove to warm up for dinnertime. We just had a bit o' bread and jam and gingerbread, but mother had a real good dinner for us when we came home at night—tatie hash and stews!'' At Rydal, "my sister and I took food to Ambleside school in a little dinner basket. When my sister fried bacon for breakfast, she would put in a little extra and make sandwiches. Sometimes we had fried egg sandwiches. We had a tin of tea or cocoa, or whatever we fancied, and the teacher set it on an old-fashioned stove to keep warm.'' A recollection from Little Langdale is of the period when "they made a big pan o' cocoa at dinnertime. We took a few coppers each week to cover the cost.'' In Kentmere, "I took bacon sandwiches, and perhaps an apple and a pear. There'd be lemonade or some tea to drink. I didn't hunger.''

Some of the children were ill-clad; most of them wore clogs. "My mother had been a dressmaker when she lived at Caldbeck, and she made me gym slips and blouses. Such a lot of girls in those days wore white pinafores with frills round. There were buttoned clogs for girls.'' One schoolgirl visited the Bridge House at Ambleside when repairs to her clogs were necessary. Here a man named Cullingworth worked. "If a caulker had come off your clogs, you went in and he put you one on while you waited. If you'd walked from Rydal to Ambleside—as I had—you would be quite happy to sit down for a while!''

It was a period when slates were used for writing. The pencils made squeaky noises as they moved. "You cleaned a slate with a cloth, and washed it now and again. You had to get it thoroughly dry before you started again, or it wouldn't show. They soon got on to paper...'' At Ambleside, "we had 'rithmetic, composition, drawing, reading. I was always a grand 'summer'. Anyone who was first with the answer when some mental arithmetic was given, late in the day, could get out of school early; I was nearly always 'first out'.''

The teachers demanded perfection. "There were three teachers in Ambleside, and we got the cane if we were late. We stood in a line just within the door and—whack, whack!'' The scholars assembled in the playground and marched into school in orderly ranks. "Sombody played the piano as we walked in.'' When 100 children were on the register at Coniston School, the head-master was John William Rich, "a real old-fashioned school-master, very strict.'' He "turned out some good scholars over the years.'' At Chapel Stile, Thomas Fisher was "good with a stick... He would deliver half a dozen strokes at a session.'' Kentmere's schoolmistress, Grace Hetherington, was generally very kind, but would administer punishment with the cane for "talking''. Kentmere school, like many others, "has given over now.''

A farmer's son in Little Langdale was "never late for school once'', though he did not live far away. "You see, I'd two cows to milk, and I'd a quarter of a mile to go to feed two young cattle. Mother wouldn't let me go to school till I'd washed, changed and put on some clean clogs." Two sisters at Wall End, Langdale, walked over three miles to and from school. Then: I'd to get the coals in. My sister got the kindling sticks. She did the ducks, and I did the hens. We had about eight calves to feed. In winter-time, we put two great bucketfuls of potatoes out and gave them to the cows—it was first world war, and we couldn't get much cake—and after father and them fed cows wi' potatoes, we'd another two buckets of potatoes to cut. We didn't have any time for homework, and we didn't have much playtime."

When illness was experienced, "you had your own remedies. No doctor was sent for; he charged a guinea a time. They didn't usually send for t'doctor until somebody was actually dying." The Tysons, of Dalehead, were a case in point. Ned Tyson met Old Dr Johnson. "He stopped and said: 'Well, how are you, Mr Tyson?' Ned replied: 'I'm not telling thee, for last time thou axed me how I was, you sent me a bill for seven and a tanner." Linseed poultices were considered good for "blood poisoning", noted for "drawing things". Poultices were made of bread, soap, even sugar. "Soft brown's the best... One chap had so many boils he said he was going to see the doctor. A friend told him: 'I'll cure you.' He made a poultice of brown sugar and soap, slapped it round his neck, and he nivver had any boils after that."

Church-going was obligatory. A farm man at Grange-in-Borrowdale regularly cycled to and from church at Rosthwaite. At Troutbeck, "you did nothing but what you were forced on a Sunday. You went to church twice a day. My father would not allow us to yoke a horse in the cart." The churchfolk "were scornful of the chapel people, and vice versa." The churches were first-rate meeting places for young people; many a marriage sprang from a friendship established after church or chapel. "That's how boys and girls git mixed up i' those days. I can just see us now, at t'top o' t'hill, coming oot o' Kentmere church, and all talking together, then setting off to go home. Only time a lad saw a lass was at t'week-end. Girls were nivver allowed out hardly through t'week. My wife lived at t'next farm at Troutbeck, about 300 yards from my spot. I came same way home from church, and as it happened there were only the two of us going that way. That's how we got to know each other." At Bampton, "I got my husband in the church choir! Vicar used to say: 'I've got a courting choir—four lads, four lassies.'"

There were energetic suitors, such as the lad living at West Head, Thirlmere. "He walked over t'tops, you know. He went over t'fell to Grasmere, then over t'next fell and met his girl at the top of Lingmell. He wouldn't have much time off—Sunday neet, likely." If lads from Shap started looking for lasses at Bampton, the Bampton boys put them in a 'calf pen'; they

'hull'd 'em'." This consisted of blindfolding the visitors and keeping them at the middle of a field. They could not remove their blindfolds because their hands were tied behind their backs! Dances were another opportunity for a boy to meet girl.

Farm servants generally married during Whit-week, when the men were due to have a week's holiday. A wedding was a time when the normal monetary restraints were waived. "They splashed out a bit. Church gates were tied; money was thrown to the youngsters." In Great Langdale, "they often put a rope across the road, and it was lucky if someone got a piebald horse and blocked the way with it." A lucky few were able to go on honeymoon, popularly to Blackpool and Morecambe. In Whitcham Valley: "we went to Morecambe for our honeymoon. Three of us in one family were married in the same year, and only me and my husband went on a honeymoon." A Great Langdale memory is of couples who simply went into the next dale and stayed with relatives. "We never got a honeymoon. There'd been illness at home. We were lucky to have the wedding..." At Bampton, "I didn't have a honeymoon at all. We were married one day, and my husband was working on the next day."

Life was divided between sleep and work, with hardly any leisure-time. "We worked all hours, and any sport was home-made. "We'd throw hats in for wrestling, and on a Sunday afternoon some of the local farmers would come along to watch us. Quoiting was very popular, and to give the police a bit of a job we'd have pitch and toss!" In Upper Lunesdale: "We met in t'village, and used old horse-shoes for quoits. There was a stone heap, and we used to sit there and play nap. There was a lot o' napping, and a lot o' whanging horse-shoes round. You just made your own fun." In one Cumbrian parish: "We wrestled in a field, or just played around, tantalising anyone who came by."

Dales dances were lusty affairs, the music being provided by fiddle or melodeon, in premises which were most varied in their size and suitability. In St John's School, between the Vale and Naddle, there was not really enough room for any activity apart from dancing, so the building containing the hearse was taken over as a supper room, the horse-drawn vehicle being pushed outside. The barn at Bridge End Farm was often used for dancing, supper being served in the house itself. One of the bedrooms served as a cloakroom. In Borrowdale, before the Institute was built, dances took place in the school or in a building near the *Royal Oak* , which belonged to the "Mechanics". For music, "Joe Jenkinson played the fiddle and blind Joe Plaskett the concertina." It cost a shilling to attend such a dance. If supper was provided, the charge went up to 1s. 6d.

The winter was enlivened by hunt suppers, merry neets or straight drinking at the nearest hostelry. Someone who overindulged was said to have been "on the spree". Young men once crossed the fells from Langdale to drink at the *Royal Oak* in Borrowdale. "One night, as they returned, they saw a cottage in Langstrath and noticed a bracken stack. They blocked in the windows of the cottage with bracken. Much later, some men who were going to the fell noticed the blocked windows and pulled away some of the bracken, rousing the man and his wife, who were "terribly capped". They had slept "two neets and a day." A quarryman who followed a fell road on a dark night knew there was a gate across that road. At what he thought was the right place, he put out a hand to detect it. The hand went between two bars, and his nose hit the gate. He entered a local inn with a blooded nose, remarking: "It's first time I knew my nose was longer than my arm!"

Heavy drinking was common when a pint of ale cost only three-pence. One man poured beer on to his breakfast porridge. Another, who regularly visited Ambleside from his home in Langdale, used a horse-drawn trap. He had so much to drink, he returned kneeling in the trap, and had such a bad attack of cramp he had to be assisted to leave. Some quarrymen stayed at lodgings on Honister for a week at a time. One man, named Gregg, remained at these high-lying lodgings for four years. He stored the sovereigns he earned in small tins. When he had over £500, he returned to civilisation. The quarryman bought himself a horse and trap. He became a spree-drinker. As his money dwindled, he sold the trap, and rode on horseback. He disposed of the gear, then the horse. Finally, he was seen walking up by Lodore with a bridle over one arm. Someone offered him 3s. 6d for it, and he accepted. After two years "on the spree" he returned to work on Honister.

The winter gloom was relieved by the celebration of Christmas, though "there was not a big lot on. Folk sometimes had parties. Christmas Day at some farms was mair or less like any other day. They had a fowl for dinner, and maybe Christmas pudding, with brandy sauce." The postman fared well, being offered a drink at every farm. One man found it impossible to mount his cycle after "I tummelled off at bottom o' t'brow." In Great Langdale, "we had one postman who on his way back stopped at Skelwith Bridge and made up with Old Swannie Wilson, a noted character. They had a bit to drink. They daren't walk down the hills, and so they slid down 'em. By the time they got back to Ambleside, they had worn their breeches bottoms out." They used to do a lot of napping (a card game) at Christmas.

In Little Langdale, "you used to have a chicken, or a bit o' pork or beef. We didn't have Christmas cake. We used to hang our stockings up, and we'd find an orange and an apple and a few nuts. Then one Christmas I got a lile toy—a celluloid duck. I thought it was marvellous." Another time, he received "a fella's face in a lile glass thing. There were five lile teeth rattling about, and you had to get them teeth into holes where mouth was." At another farm, "we had a lovely Christmas dinner—roast goose or turkey. Ours was usually a goose because my father liked it best. We had a big plum pudding, and a bowl of rum butter for Christmas tea."

A barrel of beer was purchased from Keswick for the Christmas festivities at Seathwaite. "I once got a rabbit in my stocking. Actually, it was in a big box at foot o' t'bed. I had wanted it, so I got it. I remember it was a black buck. Dad said it was cruel to keep it. I let it off—in 1913. There's still some black rabbits in Steel Wood!"

For the winter nap-parties in Great Langdale, a "gang" of men arrived at Wall End, Middle Fell and Mill Beck, had their supper, settled down to play, and maybe arose to return home next morning, as the farm children were getting ready to go to school. "Maybe before you went to bed, you made up some sandwiches. The fire was on. The men got some tea before they set off for home. They napped all night!"

In due course, a dale was saddened by news of a death. "In those fellhead spots, if anybody was ill and likely to die, they all generally knew about it. News of a death passed round, and they soon found out when t'funeral was." At Rydal: "Once or twice they came for one of my brothers to go round and bid people to the funeral. He'd go to the various houses, say that so-and-so had died, and the family wished them to come to the funeral. In Great Langdale: "They used to go round 'bidding'. It was first world war that faded that lot off. It was a foregone conclusion that every house would be represented by one person, at least, and on funeral day all t'curtains were drawn."

But first there was the viewing of the corpse, in a room at the house where the mirror was covered. (It was unlucky to glimpse a corpse through a mirror). In Little Langdale: "When anyone died, mother used to take us to the house on the night before they closed the coffin. I had seen a few dead folk before I left school. You were told to place your hands on the brow of the dead person, and if you did this you wouldn't dream about it afterwards. It didn't bother us kids." A Great Langdale memory is of the death of a baby. "Several of us kids went to the door and said: 'Please, we've come to see your baby.' The mother took us upstairs, and there was this little thing lying in a coffin. She said: 'Put your hand on its forehead.' And this we did."

At the beginning of the century, an old woman made sure that a bag or case containing her funeral wear was handy. Such wear was often beautifully made, the white "nightdress" being embroidered. At Bampton, "when Fanny Moffatt died, we found—underneath her bed, in a basket—a tape (to hold the mouth closed), scissors, socks, nightdress and handkerchief, also a piece of material to keep the feet together. There were also two pennies for her eyes.''

On funeral day, "my brother drove the old-fashioned hearse at St John's in the Vale. I remember he was very busy during the bad influenza epidemic just after the first world war. Being at the farm nearest the church, he had to take the hearse. It was a black box, on four wheels, embellished round the top.'' In Little Langdale: "We used to enjoy a funeral when we were kids. You got a ride out. I remember when my grandmother was buried, me and my brother sat wi' t'driver up on t'hearse. We thought it was a wonderful day out.'' In Mardale, the bereaved family might provide the horse that hauled the parish hearse. "There was a lot of reverence about funerals then. The bereaved family wore black for a year, in public. I remember when grandfather died, my sister and I had to have black hats, shoes, stockings, frocks and jackets. The lads had black arm bands.''

A funeral was followed by a special tea. "In Big Langdale, it was a damned good meal, with sandwiches, currant pasty and cake.''

Shippon and Dairy

THE SHORTHORN was the major milk breed. A Kentmere farmer recalls: "It was a bonny cow, red or white or a mixture, which was roan. All sorts o' shades, but usually delicate. There was nothing prettier than a roan, with its gentle colours." Around Buttermere, "a roan cow always made the most money. They wouldn't have white 'uns." At Sawrey: "T'Shorthorn should never have bin done away wi'. It'll allus be my favourite." Near Coniston: "They were Shorthorns at this farm then, and they're Shorthorns now. I've tried the others, but I've gone back to Shorthorns every time. A Shorthorn's good to look at, and I always reckon you can keep three Shorthorns to every two back-and-white 'uns."

The dairy herd was relatively small. A farmer bought or borrowed a bull, keeping some calves as replacements. "You kept a bull for 'appen three years—till he'd be mating with his immediate offspring. At times, you thought you'd made a good choice o' bull, but then it fared badly." A farmer liked to see a bull with horns "set right", extending outwards and turning inwards at the top. In Kentmere, "we usually bought bulls. There musn't be kin-breeding, so you'd probably go to Penrith and buy a bull there. Or take a trip into Yorkshire. You must keep the strains clear."

A Borrowdale farmer "bought a bull at Cockermouth, fetched it on t'train to Keswick, and walked it from Keswick to Seathwaite. What precautions you took depended on what age it was." In the west: "Not many people kept bulls, and folks used to take their cows to 'em. They walked their stock for miles." A farmer at the head of Buttermere took his surplus cows to Cockermouth, making an overnight stop, and arranging to be at the auction mart early on Monday morning so that he had a good position in the sale.

"Beastings", the custard-like flush of milk produced by a cow on calving were made into an appetising pudding. Subsequent milk was fed to the calves three times a day, and in due course a calf's diet consisted of skimmed milk and linseed. It was often the servant girl's job to feed the calves. "In the old hand-milking days, a good man was supposed to milk 12 cows in an hour. He had to be careful not to be caught by a muck-button (dried dung) on a cow's tail.

You just turned your cap round and either put the end of the cow's tail between your cap and the cow's flank, or you tied the tail round its leg if it was one of those switchin' kind." At Troutbeck: "In winter, you milked and foddered and mucked out in a morning and evening. You were always there, you know." One feature of the shippon, or cow-shed, was the greeap (group), "where t'muck goes." A carter visiting a saw-mill at Skelwith Bridge told the owner one day: "I never knew that Tom Kirby grew grapes... he telled me he wanted some sawdust for his greeaps."

The three-legged stool on which the milker sat was known as a copy; "you could buy 'em at t'Co-op i' Gurt Langdale." A local farmer insisted on having a four-legged copy. "Now and again I milked a cow outside. I were too idle to take it in! I went wi' t'pail an' copy and a bit o' cake in a tin." Some farmers had milk rounds. At Rydal, "my father used to get up about 5.30. We got up soon after, because my sisters and I milked as well and then we went round the village with the milk, twice a day. In the first world war, we charged three ha'pence a pint. We took milk in churns, in a horse and float, and measured the milk straight into the customers' jugs."

In Little Langdale, "we always grew turnips for t'stock. Turnips and hay and husks of corn—it was called 'semground' (semi-ground)—and linseed cake, were all mixed up. Linseed cake came in big slabs; I've cracked it many a time. I used to slit a piece in a cake-cracker and twine it. It was damned hard work for a lad. You put linseed in tubs, among turnips and stuff. You soaked 'chop' (chopped straw), and horses needed it short. Cows had to have it with a bit o' length and then they could fetch it up to chew. You could alter t'length on t'chopper." At Sawrey: "We grew oats and turnips for t'cows. We didn't chop turnips up for milk cows; they got 'em whole, and champed 'em up on their own. A cow'd soon scoop a turnip, I'll tell you. We just threw two or three in t'boose head, an' they scooped 'em therselves."

The farmers at the head of Great Langdale did not do a great deal of ploughing, but the best land was turned to grow potatoes, turnips, oats, even carrots—all being used on the farms. The farmer at West End made himself a flail, and used it to remove the chaff from the grain. The wooden head of the flail was connected to the shaft by leather, "nailed on each side". A double floor was used, being called a "threshing bit". It ensured that the ordinary floor would not be damaged by the whacking of the flail. Grain treated to the flail was usually riddled, and the chaff added to food placed in the cow tubs or the horse troughs. In 1918, when a man was staying at the farm, he suggested that the farmer might buy a thresher, and one was bought—a simple but robust device. "Two men twined handles at each side, and one fed in the sheaves. It was jolly hard work."

A Shorthorn was a relatively healthy beast. Each farmer needed to know about a few diseases, and the small size of the milk herd enabled him to spot ailments in good time. "I yance made a mustard plaster for pneumonia. Aye—brown paper on t'kitchen table, with a dollop of hot mustard. I just clapped it on t'cow near it's lungs. I can remember quite a few cases of pneumonia, and mustard plasters being used, and there was never a cow lost. Mind, t'cure took a long time." Another farmer "got a gurt sheet o' brown paper, size of a mat, and covered it ower wi' mustard—soft mustard, you know—and slapped it round its ribs. An' get a bottle o' summat for it to drink. By gum, it got better; it cured it!"

For mastitis, "we rubbed tits wi' t'kind o' salve t'vet gave us." Abortion was feared; a whole herd could be affected in short time. At Sawrey: "We never had anything o' t'sooart till we took this farm on our own, and then it started right away. Abortion. Ivvery cow did it, bar one, and that was a white one. It nearly finished us off. We hadn't mich money, and we were owing a bit. Landlord was very good about it. He said we could pay back when we could. He didn't charge us any interest on the debt, so that was something..." Another farmer observed: "We kept a donkey yance ower, but it didn't do any good." One man, in desperation, kept a goat in the byre, and another hung some Epsom salts above the door. "They could do nothing really." Then there was the celebrated "wooden tongue" ....

Medicines at a farm in Little Langdale were to be found in the "spice cupboard", in the kitchen. It was "vet cupboard, for cow medicines and all that." Among the items were castor oil, brimstone and treacle. "Treacle was a good medicine. We got it at t'grocers in a stone jar, 14 lb at a time. If a cow had a stoppage, we gave it beer and tracle or castor oil. We made a concoction up. If often worked. And in any case, you couldn't be having a vet coming all t'way ...." Some medicines were administered by way of a large cow horn. At Seathwaite: "An old man came round and took the loose teeth out of the heifers."

No one hears of John's Disease now. "Cattle wi' that scoured and wasted away. It seemed to go when folk started putting a lot o' lime on t'land." Other cures included lacerating the dewlap of a cow to admit a tape on which mustard was placed; the tape was periodically moved round. Sticking a knife through the thinnest part of a cow's tail was said to cure 'worm in t'tail'. "I could nivver mak oot what t'old chaps meant by it!"

Scarcely any milk left the farm as milk. It was converted into butter or, much less commonly, into cheese. The womenfolk made the butter, with help from a man on churning day. Milk was poured into bowls, which were left on a slab of stone in the milk-house for "three meals", and then the cream was carefully removed. In Borrowdale, one farmer's wife used a cow horn. The "blue milk" was fed to the young stock. At Bootle: "Grandmother used to set it up in bowls wi' spouts on. You poured milk out through t'spouts, and cream stopped behind. We carried t'milk into t'house, siled it and separated it wi' one of those proper separators you twined." At Rydal, where bowls were used, "mother was usually the one that creamed 'em. She held a bowl up and loosed the edges of the cream with a finger, then blew if off into a cream pot." The bowls were "brown outside, yellowish inside. You didn't want 'em too big or you couldn't lift 'em." Milk "leads" (galvanised containers) were in use in Kentmere.

At Bampton, "we got the lads on churning." If the soured cream was too warm in summer for successful churning, "we put t'cream pot in a container of water we'd brought from a cold spring." In Kentmere, "kitchen where we did separating, and where t'cream pot stood, faced north, and sun didn't shine into it. Everything was cold and clean." Churning could be prolonged in summer. "I used to go to my uncle's. He milked summat like 30 cows. Monday morning was for churning, and he'd one of these big, beggering things that made 60 pounds o' butter at a time. It was murder, twining the thing! In hot weather, it could take an hour and a-half or even two hours to 'turn'... Odd times, not much happened. If it was thundery weather, it was very difficult to make anything of..."

At a farm in St. John's Vale which supplied the *Royal Oak* in Keswick, and several other busy places, the butter production per week peaked at 95 lb. "The week we totalled 95 lb it was summer time, and very hot. We got up at night and did half of it; then we did the other half early next morning, before the sun had got up." In Little Langdale: "Sometimes, it took a long time to 'turn'. We used to curse it!"

Scotch Hands were used to shape up the butter into saleable portions. At Bampton: "You had to have a wooden bowl and beat the butter against the side to get the water out and mix salt in; at Chapel Hill they had a butter-worker." A skilful butter-maker adorned an oblong block of butter with a pattern imparted by the edge of one of the Scotch Hands. Where "round pounds" were made, they would be adorned with a distinctive marker, which left the imprint of a thistle, a cow or a rose. In the Whitcham Valley: "We made our butter into little round pounds; we had a print and put a picture of a cow on top of each pound. Mother had a few other patterns—thistles and things." In Little Langdale, "mother used to do the old-fashioned rolled pounds because she couldn't get the hang of patting it up. She had a butter bowl, and worked the stuff by hand to get the butter-milk out. You could hear it going 'plop-plop, plop-plop'. When she'd finished, she had a bonny round pound."

Butter was sold locally, being collected by a grocer or delivered to a grocer, and money did not often change hands. The amount earned through butter-making was deducted from the grocer's monthly account for provisions. Kentmere farmers delivered butter to the Threlfall brothers, of Staveley. A farmer in the Whitcham Valley took his butter to Millom Co-op, and from Seathwaite butter was consigned—by horse and trap—to Bowden's, in Lake Road, Keswick. There were several large grocers in Penrith who "collected butter and cheese and eggs."

Base Brown, from Grasmere, toured Great Langdale and collected butter and eggs in a square, horse-drawn van with shelves. Tom Chew, the butcher, arrived from Grasmere with a similar type of cart. "You always brought something; you didn't let him come for nothing." Jimmy Pearson, of Crosthwaite, arrived in autumn with damsons, apples, potatoes, carrots and turnips. He stayed overnight at Stool End.

At Crook, two days of each week at one farm were devoted to the making of cream cheese. A 12 oz. size was produced costing 1s.6d, but the more popular size was 6 oz, which retailed at 8d. "Cream was separated from the milk and salt was added. It was hung in a close calico cloth for the whey to drip, and then pressed solid." A design was put on top of the cheese, which was then encased in a small piece of muslin. In Mardale, "we used the surplus of milk at times to produce cheese. There was a zinc bath, which we kept in the middle scullery, for this purpose."

A girl, hired at Ulverston, developed a strong dislike of farmhouse cheese. The "missus used to make big round 'uns. She kept saying to me: 'Now taste it—in case there isn't enough salt in it.' I didn't touch cheese after leaving that farm!"

In the Hayfield

BEFORE THE MACHINES took over, men felled the meadow grass by ley (scythe). It was straight-shafted, with a blade up to six feet in length. Within living memory, a team of scythesmen moved across nearly 100 acres at Threlkeld Hall. It was soft ground, unhandy for machines. "Up yon district (upper Kentmere) they'd given up mowing by scythe when I was a nipper, just afore t'first world war, but it still went on at some of t'high fell farms." Quarrymen living in Little Langdale were experts with the ley. "I've heard fadder tell o' 20 men going down New Close, a meadow at back o' t'school, with a scythe apiece. They were felling some grass afore going to work." A Borrowdale man was loyal to his scythe even after the coming of the machines. "He loved mowing hill-ends and dyke-backs."

A man "tore himself i' bits if he didn't know how to keep a blade sharp. He had a strickle—a piece o' wood, wi' flat sides and a shaped handle. It fastened on t'shaft, and balanced it properly. My uncle made his own strickle, and he pitted it with holes, smeared wi' pitch and then shook fine, hard sand ower it. His ley-blade was like a razor, it was that sharp." Farmer Coates, of Grange-in-Borrowdale, hired a man and sent him down to the lake edge early one morning to mow some grass. A local said to the farmer: "Did thoo hear t'corncrake?" "Nay," said the farmer, "it's that farm man o' mine; he's doon at lake edge sharpening his scythe."

In Little Langdale: "There was a terrible storm one summer, just after I left school. Storm flattened a meadow. One fair morning, dad said: 'Come on, yon field's in a terrible state. Thee an' me's gang to mow it.' Talk aboot punishment. It was nearly six acres. For two or three days, I was that sore round ribs I hardly dare breath—an' I was a grown lad. Then I was all reet." An Ambleside man chatted to an old farm man he met near Loughrigg." He says: 'Thoo sees yan lile field theer?' A good few acres. 'When I was a lad I was 14th man going down there wi' a ley'."

The horse came into its own at haytime. If the weather was sunny and hot the horses would be roused "gey soon". Haytime did not begin until the third or fourth week in July—"we were clipping in July as a rule"—and with the sheep being kept in the meadows until quite late, a long dry spell could be disastrous, producing little grass to be converted into hay. "If you got a good wet time, with sunshine and showers, you got some good crops." It was frustrating for the farmers if the date of a compulsory sheep-dipping occurred on a good hay day, for notice had been given. The local policeman could, if he wished, turn up to ensure that the dipping was in accordance with the legal requirements. "You couldn't do two things at once; next day it could be raining, and your hay would be wet..."

As machines became more numerous and varied, the farm horses had their energy taxed. In Kentmere: "My father liked to be up early for mowing. One time, he came back from Brockstone clipping. There'd been a party, then a dance. Father had t'hosses in by 2.30 in t'morning. He yoked 'em up—and as soon as it was light enough to see, away they went!" In Troutbeck, "there was many a day when you had your horses in the shafts of the mowing machine, and fed with oats, as it came light. As soon as you could see across t'field, you began to mow."

The horses were the kings of the meadow, "and t'best of 'em stood between 15 and 16 h.h. We once bought a good work horse, maybe 10 years old, for £12. Horses were getting past their best when they were 20 years old, though I've mown with a horse that was 30. During haytime, you had to humour the horse a bit. A horse would be yoked up at three or four o'clock in the morning; it would be baited and rested now and again, but it might be eleven o'clock at night before it was taken out of its harness and allowed to sleep."

Near Coniston: "I always said there was nothing did as much for a horse as a tractor. It was cruelty in haytime the way horses had to work, out of one implement into another, practically night and day. After the tractors came, our last horse did next to nothing. I sometimes had it in the trap. Oh, but it had a grand life!"

An upper Lunesdale farmer bought one of the new-fangled side-delivery machines in April, and by May he could not restrain himself; he must see how it worked. He ordered his men to bring hay from the barn and they strew it across the corner of a field. The farmer harnessed his horse to the side-delivery and went happily, backwards and forwards, "rowing-up" the hay. In Heltondale, "we usually started cutting at 6.30, before t'sun got up. Horses were usually in good condition at that time of the year. After a few hours work, you would loose 'em out and give them their feed. They grazed a bit. Then you'd harness them to the 'turner' and they would go on and on."

At a Borrowdale farm: "We've machines for everything nowadays, but when I was young we even had to 'scale' the hay by hand; we weren't allowed to have forks. I've been so stiff through bending down that I've hardly been able to walk down-stairs next morning." Extra help was recruited. In some peripheral areas, Irishmen were taken on for the month, receiving their food, keep and a few pounds in cash. In upper Lunesdale, "nearly all the haytime men were Paddies. They used to hire 'em at Hawes or Bentham. Some of 'em walked to Mass at Kendal. They wouldn't miss going to Mass. If it wasn't right haytiming weather, some of 'em got tight and were locked up... they liked being paid in notes, and didn't want to be troubled by income tax!" At Rydal, "farmers were more particular than they are today. You had to rake up to the hedges. Nothing was wasted."

In very dry weather, the workers might see a whirlwind cross the meadow. "They looked to see which way round it was going. If it was going opposite way round to t'sun, they needn't worry. If it was same way round, they must look out—it would rain."

The haytime labourers did not go short of food or drink. At Sawrey, Mrs Heelis (Beatrix Potter) "bought a barrel o' beer. I never touched it. I wasn't a teetotaller, or anything like that, but I couldn't stick it when I was hot. It used to make me feel so dead. I liked a pint at night, when we'd finished." In the Troutbeck Valley, "five or nine gallon barrels of beer were bought from a brewery at Kendal for haytime drinking. The best beer cost a shilling a gallon, but haytime beer could be bought for eightpence a gallon. It was taken to the field in stone bottles; the men drank as they wished."

Gallons of botanic beer were made. The farmers' wives also had their own way of making lemondade. "I always took a big can of cold tea to the field; well, it was hot when I set off!" Drinkings (or "ten o' clocks") was an opportunity to have a bite and a drink at the changeover period. "You should have finished mowing for t'sun by 10 o' clock. They'd bring out a tea can and a lile basket with food." The main meal, at around noon, was usually eaten at home. "Tea would be a bite and a sup in the field, about 3.30. Sometimes you got same sort o' food as you'd had in t'house, but you were sitting behind a wall in t'shade eating it."

Much of the effort went into making and breaking out "cocks", some of which stood for days in chancy weather. Haytime began in July, and it was rare indeed if it ended in the same month. At Rydal, "I had four brothers and three sisters. I remember when we were working in the meadows in front of Rydal Hall when a big circus had come to Ambleside. We could faintly hear the noise, and wished we could get done so that we could go and enjoy it. When we were turning swathes, or whatever we were doing in a row, father always went first; he was never in a hurry, and would pick up a bit of hay and shake it out. And we were itching to get done, and get to the milking, so that there was still time to go to Ambleside."

In Troutbeck Valley, "we only once finished hay in July. It was t'last day. Once I got off t'mowing machine to go and play football. Haytime had lingered on till September, and I remember there was last little bit to mow below t'house. Boss was on t'football committee. He said: 'I think you're picked to play today.' I said: 'I'm not going to leave this.' He said: 'You'd better. I'll finish it off.''

In Great Langdale: "There was an old fellow, who'd loaded his last load of hay. It was the finish of haytime. He said: 'A shower reight now would do a power o' good. He got his shower! Water was running out of the cart before he got home.'' There was a delightful custom in this valley. "When you got your last load, you gave a halloa, like at a fox hunt. Then other families knew you had finished haytime. It was a matter of pride to finish first, though I suppose there were some folk who'd think: 'They must have rushed it!'''

After haytime came the harvest. A Great Langdale farmer's son was ploughing stubble in the valley when he was 12 years old. "They always had a bit o' green crop. In 1917, I was off school for three weeks for the harvesting. It was a very bad summer. Harvest was late. We finished leading grain one Saturday in October. It was 1.30 a.m. when we finished. We got last field, bar for one row of stooks beside the dyke; the wind couldn't get at it, and it was not quite ready. Father said: 'They're not properly dry, so we'll leave 'em, Next morning it was pouring down. Them stooks never were got.''

Horse Power

THE HORSE was the master of field and dusty road. Old William Hully, of Orton, said he lived "just on the division between Clydesdales and Shires". This son of a local butcher was one of those who kept an entire (uncastrated stallion), and his prize animal was *Comet*, which came originally from Stainmore and died at the age of 30 years. "I led him for 20 years on the same piece of ground, and he was serving 160-odd mares a season. He weighed 11 cwt, and could trot a mile in three minutes. If he could come back today, he would clear all before him at shows. I never had a pony that could gallop as fast as old *Comet* could trot!"

A man with an entire had his regular rounds during the season. "A chap called Tommy Burns travelled Kilpatrick's horses, from Wigton. He'd set off in t'morning and put up at various places en route. One entire from Wigton finished up at Millom, and then he used to 'train' back to yon end, and start again on Monday morning. They never travelled on Sundays, but one stallion was put up in a big loose-box at the *King's Head* in Bootle, and quite a lot of farmers took their mares there on Sunday morning!"

At Sawrey: "Entires came round here every week. We had three foals one year. I remember a chap from Whitcham Valley; he charged £2 a time, and if it didn't take, you only paid the groom's fee. He brought round a bonny one, but another was an ugly devil, and I didn't like it. He put up somewhere in Hawkshead." The man who toured with an entire was not allowed to ride, "cept last journey home." The entire season started in May and finished at the end of June. It is noted that "them chaps who travelled entires never got as much money as a good cowman; they were nearly always chaps who were keen on their beer." A Kentmere farmer took his mare to Kendal, "and met the entire at back of one of the hotels." The farmers at the head of Langdale went to Park Farm, which was visited by an 'entire' belonging to Moses Edmondson, of Ulverston. He employed a man to lead the animal around, and they were in the dale once a week during the season.

The Midland Railway Company kept the biggest horses in the neighbourhood of the Settle-Carlisle line. "They were gurt cross-bred Clydesdales." Other notable horses were owned by the big

65

hotels; a number were sold off at the end of the tourist season, and local farmers were keen to buy them. Coaches operated over Kirkstone Pass, one of them being driven by a man called Willan, whose nickname was Lons. "I went with him when I was a lad. I had to nip off the coach at top of a hill and put a 'slipper' under the rear wheel to lock it." This primitive form of braking was frowned on by the highway authorities. It left a channel in the comparatively soft surface of the road. "I sat on the box-seat with the coachman, and he used to hand me the reins—also known as ribbons—while he cut up his twist for a smoke."

There was a procession of four-in-hands on the scenic Round which took in Buttermere and Newlands Vale, beginning and ending at Keswick. As many as eight horse-drawn coaches were in view at one time. The livery testified to their ownership by a number of well-known hotels. "Drivers didn't draw wages. They collected a shilling for every passenger. Me and some pals earned money by walking over Honister towards Buttermere. We stood beside the road, waiting for a coach to arrive. A 'slipper' had been put under a back wheel at the top of the hill. Where the road levelled out, someone had to pick up that slipper and hang it on the coach. Lads rushed to pick up a slipper. Friction made it hot, and sometimes it had to be splashed with water from a bucket. Passengers tossed coins to anyone who helped, and sometimes I made as much as 5s a day. I was lucky, really. An uncle drove one of the coaches!"

Some of the finest horses pulled the coaches belonging to "Dickie" Riggs of Windermere. Also remembered are three Ambleside families, the Browns, Bells and Taylors. A splendid outfit was kept at the *Prince of Wales* at Grasmere. Incidentally, Mr Riggs was a prominent Liberal. "When I was a schoolgirl, his photograph hung in the homes of all good Westmorland Liberals. Then he married a Conservative, and everyone took the photographs down!"

Old John Wilman, of the *Royal* at Kirkby Lonsdale, kept a large stable, and owned a variety of vehicles. There was not much work for horses in winter, so he loaned them out, without charge, to Lakeland farmers. "I went with him one day when he was checking on the condition of some horses in Patterdale. Somebody had told him a farmer wasn't looking after them too well."

Most of the horses were engaged in farm work. It might take two or three months to break-in a working horse. "They had to get used to the bit in their mouths. Then you introduced 'em to the saddle and tracings. We used to strap a pair of old trousers, filled with straw, to a horse's back! Horses were often yoked to a log of wood, to see if they could pull."

A hard day's work was the rule. "At ploughing time, if you weren't out in t'field wi' a pair of horses at hawf past seven in a morning, it was a disgrace. (Sunday morning, you'd go round other folks's ploughing, to see which was best!). Near Coniston: "I was a lot better fellow when I followed 'osses than I was sat on a tractor." A horse at Seathwaite was known as a "kicker", and on a trip to Keswick an opportunity came for a young man to "get even" with it. It was early November, and he had bought some fireworks. He tied a "jumper" to the horse's tail. "We laughed and laughed till the thing flew off." Next day, back at the farm, grandfather wanted his horse." Then he said: 'There's a bit o' string on t'owd mare's tail. I wonder hoo it's gitten theer?' We nivver let on." The postman travelled from Keswick to Seathwaite by pony and trap. This was before the 1914-18 war. "Mother used to send the *Westmorland Gazette* to grandfather each week. Postman would be coming up Borrowdale, with his old horse trotting away—you could see him when he was a mile off—and he'd be reading t'newspaper."

The blacksmith was a jack-of-all trades, but his services were in the most steady demand by those who wished him to shoe working horses. His most exacting jobs were the shoeing of unbroken "stags" which had been bought at the autumn sales. At Kirkby Stephen, "there was a terrible carry-on when frosty weather came. All the shoes had to be taken off and sharpened. At the beginning of the century, an apprentice to the trade received one shilling a week (at Shap).

In Little Langdale, "council used to hire a horse and cart for road work. They had 'gravel 'oles' up roadsides where they got material for t'roads. They set men to work knapping stones. Two old chaps broke stones at a spot between Outgate and Hawkshead. Each had a bonny lile hammer. Poor old lads—they used to have to work hard to make a few coppers." Whinlatter was "metalled" about 1926. "At slack times, farmers contracted to cart road material to Whinlatter: eight shillings a day for horse, cart and man." When tarmac was laid at Spital Level, Kendal, "there was bedlam wi' t'farmers. They said: 'If you come up Spital Hill, we'll nivver git our groceries and stuff from Kendal. When they started to tar forward, council left a strip so wide for horses and carts to come up side of t'road." Hardknott Pass was once "looked after" by the men who farmed Black Hall and Brotherilkeld farms, and they were "paid for their trouble by the council." Beside the Struggle, the steep road from Ambleside to Kirkstone Pass, was a memorial to a dead horse. It was said of that horse that "his only fault was dying."

The springtime of 1917 was "dreadful". "It would snow and then be fine, but it always froze at night. It went on like that away into May. When it finished it was as if it couldn't snow any more." The sheep suffered, and local farmers bought in hay for the first time, collecting it from Windermere station by horse and cart, and paying about £6 or £7 for the hay. Horse-drawn vehicles were also employed to move lime. "The first lot of lime we got had to be carted from Chapel Stile. It came from above Kendal, and old Herbert Bennett and his son brought it by motor wagon from Ambleside. The year was 1923." The wagon was too cumbersome for the bridges, and so the farmers of Stool End, Wall End and Middle Fell transported it for the last few miles. "It was in big pieces; it wasn't slacked. The slacking took place when it had been spread in heaps about the field and the rain fell on it."

Farmers reckoned you could keep three cows where you kept one horse." A horse was known to "eat bare". At Sawrey: "I reckon it eats far barer than a cow, you know." It must not be provided with dusty food, or it would be "brokken-winded". A Little Langdale farmer observes: "You could fairly hear a brokken-winded 'oss. It would live on, but living must have been hard work for it."

Many a farmer had not enough time to break in a horse, and so he bought one. "Sheep and cows were my job." At Heltondale, "when you decided to sell a horse, you walked it to Penrith, and sold it through the ring at the auction mart. Then you'd buy an unbroken colt. We bought Clydesdales mainly, from the low country about Carlisle. These were just halter-broken, and you walked 'em back home." It was customary for this man to buy a colt at two and a-half years of age, break it in and wear it for a couple of years before selling it. In Kentmere: "Only the stags were run on the fell. You took care of the working horse, and kept it round the house, so that it would be handy. A horse that was working was to clean down every night. Dad saw to it that it was cleaned down properly."

A Kentmere father bred fast trotting horses, and his son had the task of riding them for exercise, "half way down the dale, over to Ings and up Troutbeck, returning over Garburn Pass. In winter, when there was snow, or a hard frost, they were exercised in a cart, collecting coal at Staveley for t'owd ladies of Kentmere."

Fell ponies have for long been part of the Lakeland scene, especially in the eastern areas. "They are something like a miniature horse; they used to do the ploughing. A Clydesdale and fell pony crossed was one of the hardiest animals on the farm. Hard as otters, they were." A fell pony was "damned near a horse, only on less legs." Fell ponies still live in a semi-wild state along the East Fellside of the northern Pennines, and groups are spread about the hills between Pooley Bridge and the head of Kentmere. Ponies cross High Street and High Raise, where they are as much at home as the sheep. "Two and a-half years is the most desirable 'breaking' age, but I've seen us break in ponies at up to seven years old. A 'desperate' pony takes longer to break than does a 'sensible' animal." Ponies, haltered but unbroken, were once shown at fairs. "It doesn't take long to break in a pony, but it is maybe 10 days or a fortnight afore you could say it was quiet. You've to wear a pony in. It'll break itself in after a while."

A farmer from Great Langdale, attending a Lakeland show, saw a "terrible lot o' fell gallowa's... A man and his wife stood near me. They were judging these fell ponies and they kept saying to yan anudder: 'I think these must be miniature shires.' I let 'em ramble on a bit, and then I said: 'Don't you know what they are?' They said: 'No, we've come down out of London, you see. I said: 'Well, them's the real proper fell pony.' They asked me what use they were. I said: 'You'd know if you were living on a farm... They can handle a machine; they can handle a plough an' aw. They are tough customers. Aye. A far tougher thing than a big 'oss."

The horse gradually gave way to horse-power. The first car to be driven in Borrowdale belonged to the Simpsons of Haael Bank; it was a brand-new Argyll brought from Newcastle in 1911 and driven by Jonathan Hind, whose official job was coachman/gardener. The first car in St John's Vale was operated by steam and belonged to Arthur Hooper. The first vehicle in a more recognised form was a Krit of 20 h.p. owned by the Chaplin family. It was purchased in 1910, when the road down the Vale was little more than a farm track. Oil lamps were fitted. The journey from Grasmere to Keswick one dark night took three hours. As the car was travelling by Thirlmere, the brother of the driver stood on the running board, holding an acetylene cycle lamp so that its rays indicated the position of the boundary wall.

The Cost of Living

JACKSON MOUNSEY, who moved to Skelwith Bridge in 1922, was a collector of taxes, at a time when income tax was sixpence in the pound. The local people paid a shilling in rates for the whole year. "The road rate was twopence in the £, and the poor rate was collected in two instalments, of sixpence and fourpence."

When gold sovereigns were "on the job", an old man in upper Lunesdale settled the local miller's account with gold. "He kept a few hens. I went with his bill one day, and it was under two quid. Course, you got quite a lot o' stuff for £2 in them days. He got an old brown purse out of his pocket, and said: 'I should have a gold sovereign in here.' He opened it, scratched round, and said: 'By Jabe, it's here.' But he couldn't get it out. It had been in his purse that long, and wi' t'pressure on it in 'is pocket, it had embedded in t'leather. He had to use a knife to dig it out!"

A dalesman born before the 1914-18 war recalls: "In wintertime, you went to each other's houses to play nap, and smoke, and sup home-brewed beer. Then they got further advanced and started supplying whisky. You could get a bottle for about 7s. 6d in 1910. Price got to 12s. 6d, and they thought it was ruinous." When, 60 years ago, a Great Langdale couple were married, they moved into a new, stone, detached house standing on a substantial plot of ground. They paid £630 for the design and construction, and £70 for the plot. The man's wage was about £3 a week, as a quarryman, and soon after his marriage he joined fellow quarrymen on strike over working conditions; the strike lasted five weeks. "Our only extravagance each week was buying a sixpenny bar of chocolate."

A man who set off with horse and cart to visit the coalyard at Braithwaite station, near Keswick, had a ten shillings note in his pocket. "I'd pick up and pay for 'appen 10 or 11 hundredweight of coal, and still have some change. I wanted it as well. We thought a lot of threepence then."

An enterprising farm lad could earn coppers by gathering "brokken wool" from dead sheep on the fell, "and that sort o' thing. I did a bit o' work on roads. We never had mich money in our pockets i' them days." In Little Langdale, "mother used to say: 'What is it toneet, lads?' We daresn't tell her a lie, and we'd say: 'A dance. Eighteenpence.' She'd give us the money. We were satisfied if we got any."

Incidents from the Great Slump are vividly recalled. "They talk about the 1930s, but I think people have forgotten about the 20s. If you were working in industry, like me, you'd go to work, stand about and then get sent back." In Great Langdale: "Top men on the farms were lucky if they could get £1 a week. Top men, mind. Lads were getting about four or five pund for t'aif year, and they had to work hard—seven days a week!" At Bampton, "my husband was earning 19s. 3d a week on a farm. That was in 1931. He got a quid really, but he had 9d knocked off for insurance. I did one or two jobs, and got 2s. 6d a week. We paid 4s. 6d a week rent—and managed to save two bob a week... We never got into debt."

After the buoyant wartime trade, the economic conditions had deteriorated and were at their worst in the early 1930s. In Great Langdale: "I remember my husband coming back from Ambleside Fair, and he says: 'Everything's gone to pot. It's a gurt slump.'" The effect on stock prices was dramatic. "Do you know, they'd have a fit, would these fellows today... Six bob a head for the very best of sheep." In the western dales: "I can always remember father going to Whitehaven dairy auction with a cow, and it made £17. I played pop with him. I'd just left school. I said: 'You should have brought it home.' He said: 'All reet, me lad, next 'un that's to go, you tak it!' So I went wi' t'next one, and came back wi' £14".

Half-bred lambs at Millom auction were being knocked down at 14s each. "I remember when nine fat Herdwick ewes made 9s. each." A girl from Whitcham Valley took green peas to sell at Ulverston. She wanted a halfpenny a pound. "Sometimes I couldn't get a ha'penny."

In Great Langdale: "I thought sheep were a handy price at £2 each in 1927, but in 1931 I couldn't sell 'em for ten bob apiece. There were no subsidies then." In the early 1930s "lile hoggs" being sold by a farmer in Little Langdale made 5s each, and wool was being sold at 2¾d a pound. "Price o' sheep didn't pick up until t'next war. Even so, when grading began, only 1s. 2d a pound was being allowed. I reckon sheep farming was at its best in 1955. It's gone downwards ever since."